RELIGION, MYTH AND THE BRAIN

RELIGION, MYTH AND THE BRAIN

✦

How Religion Began and How Modern Science Explains The Origins of Myth

George F. Bain

B.Com; M.A. (econ),

Cognitive Neuroscience Society.

Sometime Lecturer

at University of Toronto

and at George Mason University Institute for Learning in Retirement

iUniverse, Inc.

New York Lincoln Shanghai

RELIGION, MYTH AND THE BRAIN

How Religion Began and How Modern Science Explains The Origins of Myth

iUniverse books may be ordered through booksellers or by contacting:

iUniverse
2021 Pine Lake Road, Suite 100
Lincoln, NE 68512
www.iuniverse.com
1-800-Authors (1-800-288-4677)

Display courtesy of Dr. Boree, Shippensburg University, who has granted permission for their reproduction here.

ISBN-13: 978-0-595-42021-6 (pbk)
ISBN-13: 978-0-595-86364-8 (ebk)
ISBN-10: 0-595-42021-4 (pbk)
ISBN-10: 0-595-86364-7 (ebk)

Printed in the United States of America

"They will differ,
If they do,
As syllable from Sound"

Emily Dickinson

Contents

PREFACE

Why would anyone want to read another book about religion and myth? How could this one be different or even interesting? My motivation for writing this new book is to ground the presentation in the most current findings of biology and psychology and to try to explain the interrelations among myth and religion. How, for example, is religion supported and even created by myth? The new application of modern brain imaging throws new light on the interrelations noted and explains why humans have a universal tendency toward religion. Myths and other elements of religion are most likely transmitted over time and space by 'memes'—a type of cultural element that has many of the characteristics of biological evolution—and may be generated within the brain with many of the basic mythological themes unchanged.

That raises the fundamental question though as to how this can be possible. It appears that evolutionary psychology (EP), although contentious, is a new method for finding out why humans act as they do. It is also the case that new brain imaging techniques can shed light upon the question, "Why do humans at all times and ages seem to be drawn to religion?" Developed since 1975, EP is still a very new field of study. It has not yet been universally accepted as a separate discipline. It is not yet included in all standard college biology and psychology texts and it is almost certainly not included at the high school level of these studies.[1] Its birth in 1975 was seen as an attack on the then standard areas of academic interest in biology and psychology.

EP provides an alternative framework for thinking about many aspects of human nature that is just now beginning to replace traditional ways of discussing biology and psychology. The use of brain imaging has developed very recently via advances in basic science and their application to medical machinery. My hope in writing this book is that EP and the findings of brain imaging can now be related to both religion and myth.

Brain Imaging is now centered upon several sorts of technologies. Functional Magnetic Resonance imaging (fMRI) and positron Emission Tomography (PET) have been used to observe changes in brain function in many epileptic patients and in those who have offered to be 'observed' during various stages of meditation and religious activities. Some of the findings will be noted in Chapter 4.

The stories of Gods, heroes, and the journeys of heroes that we all listened to as children, or began to read ourselves as kindergartners, and referred back to during our youth, are those same stories that have fascinated many fine minds for millenniums. These myths, in some form, are common in most societies past and present. Intrigued by the similarities between the myths of many different societies, and conscious of the similar themes in religion, avid students of both have all asked, "What is the real meaning and purpose of religion and myth and why are they so closely related and intertwined?"

Lacking the most modern tools of science and its recent findings, previous investigators could only either speculate about an answer or accept without question the rules and precepts of their religion, rendering all truth to their God. Until the post World War II period, most students of religion and myth could only make shrewd guesses about the real origins and meaning of myths. Some of those suggest the answer that will be offered here. Now, however, science offers new ways to explore religion and myth using genetic information and imaging. I shall try to put the new knowledge forth toward an understanding of mythology.

A recently published book[2] seeks to explain myth by a "deconstructionist" approach to mythology. It grounds many mythical themes in natural disasters such as volcanic eruptions, earthquakes, tsunamis, and other natural events. This approach offers many possible explanations of how some myths may have been formulated. For example, in this book, the eruption of Thera, the volcano in the Eastern Mediterranean now known as Santorin, currently a tourist destination in the Aegean, was interwoven with the story of the Jewish Exodus. This is despite the obvious disparity in the dates of the two events—Thera explosion 1,500 BCE and Exodus about 1,142 or 1,462 BCE. It is not a satisfactory explanation of the events set forth in Exodus 13.22 regarding a pillar of smoke by day and a pillar of fire by night. The authors claim that the Thera event might have been visible from the route taken by the Jewish migration out of Egypt. Other of their explanations, many erudite and interesting, seem credible and rely upon tribal memories of disasters. But it is also the case that to offer a 'shock effect' explanation for mythology is not credible and does not address the question posed herein—why do mythic themes of old persist to recent days and why are these themes often associated with religion?

There have been many, many people interested in mythology, and even more who are interested in religion. Many of these have written and studied the subject, always trying to compare it to aspects of the current life of their time. Among those influential in this field are Sir James Frazer (*The Golden Bough*), Sigmund Freud (*The Interpretation of Dreams*), Carl Jung (*Man and His Symbols*), Mircea Eliade (*The Sacred and the Profane*) and, perhaps, the best known today, Joseph Campbell (*The Masks of God*). The works of these, mainly, ethnologists have faded from memory among current researchers, earning at best only passing reference, or a footnote. However, they are relevant in this work. Campbell's approach is fascinating and rather Jungian (stressing racial and cultural inheritance), an approach that, in view of recent findings in EP, is not to be dismissed out of hand in favor of more concrete explanations. There may, indeed, be a type of human memory facilitated by genetic or selective processes. One such process is named Baldwinian evolution, of which there will be more later.

Recently, there has been a revival of interest in explaining religion, perhaps driven by the attacks on science by those who cleave to Biblical explanations of religion. Among these recent discussions of religion undertaken by scientists are, for example, the works of Pascal Boyer (*Religion Explained*), David Sloan Wilson (*Darwin's Cathedral*), Daniel C. Dennett (*Breaking the Spell*), and d'Aquili and Newberg (*The Mystical Mind*), Sam Harris (*Letter to a Christian Nation*), and Richard Dawkins (*The God Delusion*).

This book evolved from several lecture series, that I gave to senior groups in the Northern Virginia area over the years from 1985 to 2003. Some of the presentations were also to church groups and along the way I became aware that few of the audiences had ever considered the relationship of religion and myth. Appendix D contains my lecture notes regarding one part of these lectures. Few in the audiences realized that many of the mythological themes currently seen in Christianity had histories going back to some 5,500 or more years before the Christian era (BCE). Moreover, most were completely unconscious of the origins of the religions in other parts of the world. The Christian churches, although active in proselytizing, are, for the most part, unwilling to recognize many similarities among various preceding doctrines and do not tend to listen to devotees of other religions. Because of my interest in EP, mythology, and science, perhaps the following will make clearer the similarities to be found in many religions through their mythology.

The material in this book will began with a review of what religion really is, in broad terms. There follows a description of evolutionary psychology and human nature; and how, in the very distant past, humans granted sentience to many things and were concerned that all aspects of nature might contain either helpful or hurtful elements. A brief discussion of animism follows and leads to the development of communication with the non-earthly powers that were assumed to control the natural world. During this and subsequent eras, the small family group and later larger groups and tribes were female centered. Because the men were mainly absent in herding and hunter societies, women maintained the groups. There followed an era of matriarchal influence that exists even today.

Surrounded by the fears and uncertainties of the world, there arose individuals claiming to have knowledge of the world. This led into shamanism that, in turn, led to structured group control. The rise of a priestly class, control of the societal centers of power and the development of rituals and hierarchy followed. Contesting the power between a growing group of leaders among a larger and widespread population, resulted in the emergence of a dominating single leader—a 'primus inter pares'—often a war leader, better suited than a priestly class to deal with issues related to cooperation within and between primitive 'societies.' All this takes humanity to just before the invention/discovery and slow spread of agriculture.

Before the spread of agriculture, the stories that supported the various societies—the myths of the time—were related to the supernatural, to the Gods that dwelt in the sky and to the demons that were below. This dichotomy—often referred to in psychological and mythological studies as the pairs of opposites[3]—stems from certain structures in the brains of all humans, so that all humans tend to have a markedly similar basic set of myths.

With agriculture, humanity had to change from a hunter-gatherer society to a more static one. The rise of patriarchy began and influenced, over time, the structure of relations between the shaman (now to be called priest) and the war leader. The effects of this were to establish a new relationship between men and women and between the priest and the leader, now called king. Humans had spread throughout the world and, carrying some traits with them, had created localized groups of religion. How that might have occurred is the subject of another part of this book, which is related to the evolutionary effects of the environment and experience upon humans. Additionally, there were times of the mixing of peoples and of clashes among those of various beliefs.

It is now possible to trace the timing and actual routes of humans as they spread about the world. It can be shown that the common traits, including some mythologies that grew in response to early experiences and the ideas of shamans, or priests, as well as the more organized religious ideas of larger societies, all traveled with humanity. Migrating, too, were basic languages that changed and developed from root languages. The book clearly shows how languages are related as well.

As to why there should be a transmission of similar ideas, I next point to recent brain imaging techniques that indicate the manner in which religious experiences are developed. A general description of the brain shows that there are similar structures with varied, specific, and general functions. These show that the ecstasy and feeling of oneness with the universe realized in many religions, and the epiphanies of religious leaders and others, all stem from the basic structures of the human brain. The need for ritual and myth is explained. The fact that all brains in humans are similar may explain why religion is both ubiquitous and why there are so many different religions. From the mutilations of the Aztecs to the tribal religions of early humans and to the communal burials of the Middle East's early religions—the very word 'religion' encompasses so many variants that it is not possible to cleave to other explanations. The commonality of myth—the stories that carry on various religious traditions—is explainable both by the common brain structures of humans and the rather evolutionary appearance of methods of genetic alteration and the appearance of 'memes' that are the instruments of the transmission of mythologies.

Readers will appreciate that I can do little more than refer to the voluminous literature on religion and myth. Although I have read hundreds of books in these fields over the past 10 years, and I have taken copious notes of items on the Internet, I have not the resources or the time to document each element beyond what is noted in the endnotes and the scant list of books. You will have to look them up yourselves or write to me for comment. Sorry about that.

Regards,

George Bain, Silver Spring, MD. 20904, December 2006
3126 Gracefield Rd. Apt 402

1

RELIGION, MYTHOLOGY AND HUMAN DEVELOPMENT

One cannot discuss mythology without understanding that it and religion are intertwined. Equally, one cannot begin to deal with the modern concepts surrounding these topics unless one has a grip on current thinking about human nature, the brain, and the new discipline of evolutionary psychology. Consequently, I want to deal with my understanding of the current attitude toward these topics as they relate to religion and mythology. What is religion and how is it intertwined with mythology? How do the new understandings relate to them and to mythology?

Religion

What is religion? How may we define it? Of many alternatives, I have chosen the one suggested by Daniel Dennett—religion is:

> *... social systems whose participants avow belief in a supernatural agent or agents whose approval is to be sought.*

This it seems to me is all-inclusive and minimal of confusion. As you read, think how this definition of religion includes the many I shall mention. There are many other definitions but few relate to how religion might have started. A posting to <evolutionary-psychology> last year provides an alternative to the schema proposed herein.[4]

Religiosity

By religiosity, I do not mean the common meaning—avid or excessive religious piety—but, rather, the structures or networks within human brains that are *receptive* to certain ideas and inputs that we now call religious. In my view, any set of ideas or inputs can be called religious IF they trigger brain elements with implications that involve four basic "instincts." These are mysticism, ritual, ethics, and myth. I will try to explain later how this may come about.

One scholar, Paul Boyer, has pointed out:

> *Culturally successful religious concepts are the outcome of selective processes that make some concepts more likely than others to be easily acquired, stored (in the brain) and transmitted. Some of the constructs of human imagination connect to intuitive ontological (metaphysical) principles in such a way that they constitute a small catalog of culturally successful supernatural concepts. Experimental and anthropological evidence confirm the salience (importance) and transmission potential of this catalog. Among these supernatural concepts, cognitive capacity for a social interaction introduces a further selection. As a result, some concepts of supernatural agents are connected to morality (ethics), group identity, ritual and emotion. These typical "religious" supernatural agents are tacitly presumed to have access to information that is crucial to social interaction, an assumption that boosts their spread in human groups* [5]

Religious concepts "tweak" the usual inferences of functionally distinctive mental systems that are also present in non-religious contexts. These mental systems deal with the detection and representation of animacy and agency, social exchange, moral intuitions, precaution against natural hazards, and understanding of misfortune. Each of these activates distinct neural resources and networks. What makes notions of the supernatural intuitively plausible? It seems to be the joint coordinated activation of these diverse systems. This opens the possibility of a neuroscience of religious beliefs.

Paul Boyer suggests that *mysticism* uses an intuitive understanding of the nature of existence or metaphysics to form the basis for dealing with reality and classifying it, so to say, into, animal, vegetable, or mineral. Supernatural experiences derive from a mix of metaphysical experiences. *Ethics* is founded on the experiences of social exchanges and ideas about reciprocity, fairness, evenness in exchange (justice), cheater detection (those who might use social exchanges for personal aims), and the "in and out" of group differentiation. *Myths* derive from language and are the expression of themes that support social bonding within a group, families and kin areas. They become the history of the group. *Rituals* make certain symbols and acts, including dance and dress, more expressive or obvious of commitment to reliable in-group morale and, by association, activate the mythological elements. In and of themselves, rituals may have the ability to activate neural networks that pull together the other elements that define religiosity.

As Boyer states, "*Religious concepts and norms and the emotions attached to them seem designed to excite the human mind, linger in memory, trigger multiple inferences in the precise way that will get people to hold them true and communicate them.*" All of these elements, including proto-language, were present during the evolution and development of *Homo sapiens.* Present, too, were the enduring mysteries occasioned by inexplicable happenings such as floods, lightning, thunder, earthquakes, etc that might be attributed to a variety of personalized forces. From this generally common situation alleviation was sought by appeal to the higher forces through rituals thought to be pleasing to them. Dancing, drumming and repetitious movements are common in all early societies as such actions were supposed to be pleasing to the higher powers. Human religiosity, consequently, emerges from the mental interaction among the elements—*ethics, mysticism, ritual, and myth.*

Boyer suggests that religiosity appears to be an adaptation in an evolutionary sense. This adaptation could be seen, I suggest in the fact that that early humans saw benefits to a small group in developing the ethics of fairness in exchange and dealings among and between groups; that the elements of the stories told and impressed upon humans by their groups became embedded upon their psyche; and that the rituals undertaken to appease the higher powers became part of the human evolutionary experience.

Aspects of culture are retained in the brain if they are rich in inferences about safety and about aspects of the environment, including other people. Such inferences were crucial to the existence of humans at the dawn of humanity. So far as I am aware, this idea of Boyer's is the first time it has been suggested that receptivity to core ideas about mythology, and the other elements noted above is adaptively embedded in the brain. This will be explored further in Chapter Four, below.

It should be noted that the foregoing applies to all religions, even those that involve bizarre practices such as human sacrifice. Some religious practices involve scarifying, head or neck stretching, burning wives, sexual orgies and the use of mind-altering herbs. Acceptance of the general description given here to religion will explain both the ubiquity and great variety of religions in the world and their many expressions of religion.

The cautions and fears of early humans made inferential ability the key to survival. Between 175,000 and 75,000 years ago when modern humans began to appear (counting from the beginning of the Common Era or BC), a basic understanding of right and wrong had been achieved through normal everyday interactions and exchanges. Religiosity was evident in the use of ocher and through burials and their attendant rituals; carvings and primitive art had been made as is revealed by numerous evidences of religious traits such as the existence of the "bear skull" altars of Neanderthals found near Nurnberg.[6] Dance, or ritual, was practiced (at least as far as can be inferred from its recent and continuing practice among aboriginals in Australia and on isolated islands). Chants and mouth music, or songs, prefaced the appearance of a mythology before the development of a complete language facility.

These evidences were followed by the appearance in very early times of specific doctrines and practices as well as by exclusivity of beliefs within the tribe, and by violence between in- and out-groups that had differing tribal structures, practices and beliefs. Because religiosity was rich in inferences and thus of value among humans for its survival benefits, it was quickly developed and became evident over the whole area of expanding human occupation. Because humans needed a great deal of information in order to make judgments that permitted them to continue to exist, they turned to the metaphysical and the mysterious for guidance. They looked thus for the meaning of present conditions and the likely future—to the waxing and waning of the moon, the change of seasons, changes in star patterns (early peoples could actually see the brilliance of the stars) and other natural mysteries.

It became evident to early humans, especially in the northern and southern hemispheres, that there was a generalized organization to the world, which was evident in the change of seasons, day lengths and appearances of the major stars. Thus, there started a recording, perhaps via marks, of the passage of days. Humans also realized that they were part of a larger system that included animals, plants and trees; and to each of these they ascribed animacy or 'aliveness.'

An early ethnographer, Sir. E.B. Tylor, in his 1871 work, *Primitive Culture*, claimed that this human trait, called animism, is the root of all religions. He believed that it was human nature to create beliefs about the world, as it was within human nature to seek explanations and assurances about the mysteries and uncertainties surrounding their lives. As we can never know with certainty what may have been the attitude of primitive humans about their belief in the universal animacy of things, I think we must accept the generally agreed stance that such was the view among humans in their state of nature.

Animism and Shamanism

In this and the following sections, I shall deal with animism, the concept of the sky god and some creation myths involving water and the egg, and with Gaia as well. This introduces the beginning of the important concept of "pairs of opposites." From this, my route leads past the magic mountain idea directly to shamanism. I next discuss growth in the tropics and in the temperate regions, introducing the influence and spread of agriculture on the beginning of religion. It is useful to recall here that temperatures varied a good deal during the period from about 20,000 years BCE until recently. These changes, mainly felt in temperature in the temperate zones but also in periods of drought in the tropic zones, caused great stress upon humans. Stress speeds up changes in the genome and the gradual acceleration of environmental stress quite likely caused both the appearance of language (the FOXP2 gene that is needed for language seems to have developed about some 40,000 years ago) and affected general intelligence levels in various parts of the world.

The following information comes from "A Review and Atlas of Paleovegitation"[7]

Past Changes in Temperate Zone Climate

14,500 years ago	Rapid warming and deglaciation begins
13,500 years ago	Climate about the same as today
13,000 years ago	Older Dryas cold phase lasting about 200 years
12,800 years ago	Beginning of intensely cold Younger Dryas, parts wetter
11,500 years ago	Previous cold ends suddenly (few decades) warm, moist
9,000–8,200 years ago	Warmer and moister than today
8,200 years ago	Sudden cold lasts 200 years

8,000–4,500 years ago	Warmer and moister than today
5,900 years ago	Sudden short lived cold phase, famine and starvation
4,500 years ago	Climates similar to present
2,600 years ago	Wet and cold period
1,400 years ago	Wet/cold period in west Europe, famines spread
700–200 years ago	Little Ice Age

The development of agriculture and the slow encroachment of this new way of life also produced stress and a general acceleration of human development. Some examples of how agriculture affected the beginning of various types of religion are given.

Themes of Early Religions

Animism

The concept of the "sacred" refers to the way in which tribal mysteries of communicating with the Gods were arranged and hidden from the general view. In some areas, markings or paintings are considered sacred. In one instance, cave paintings in Australia, made some 40,000 years ago, have been independently copied—with fidelity—by tribal members since they were originally executed. The paintings are considered sacred and their fidelity, as the copies were all made from memory of the cave art, is astounding. This is an example of the transmission of ideas from generation to generation through what is now called a "meme."

This section, dealing with animism and shamanism, relies heavily on the work of many ethnologists. For the most part, this work was done prior to 1953 and the birth of modern evolutionary psychology. The section relies heavily on the writings of Mercia Eliade and his writings, such as *The Sacred and The Profane*, *Patterns in Comparative Religion*, and *Shamanism*. I have also consulted *The Golden Bough* by Sir James George Frazer, published in 1922. There is also the four volume collection, *The Masks of God*, by Joseph Campbell. On the other works, including some e-books, mentioned in the notes, substantial quotations from those sources will be presented. I shall attempt first to deal with animism.

The core idea in animism is that each element of the natural world has a soul. The elements may be benign or evil. Many primitive religions treat the animals that are killed and eaten as having souls, or essences, that must be propitiated through making prayers to the food and the soul of the beast that provided it. This view was common in hunter-gatherer societies and in some religions such as Shinto of old. The prayers and rituals became increasingly stylized eventually involving the whole tribe.

Ancient humans were, then, surrounded by many spirits about which they must be cautious. Above them were the sky, the sun by day, and the moon and stars by night. Most primitive societies, in their belief systems, do have the concept of a sky god whose domain waxes and wanes through the year, providing a simple means of counting such as when the sun reaches its low and high points during the year. There was general unease as the sun sank lower during the year and they almost universally wondered whether it would return. As will be shown later, this concept of a 'God on high' is almost a universal among humans.

Among the inferences made by all people was that of a higher mystery or a god—often an invisible presence of someone similar to one's self but with monumental powers. A recent publication asks:

> *"How, without any physical reality on which it could be based, have those images of God or gods taken hold in the human brain?*[8] "

The scientific groundwork for an answer to that question was laid in 1890 when Sir. J. G. Frazer published the results of his anthropological study of magic and religion in his book, *The Golden Bough.* [9]With an overwhelming collection of data; Frazer showed that the idea of God had an evolutionary history. It started with the earliest human beings attempting to control their environment through magic. If you want rain, then splash water around. If you want to have success in the hunt, then dance the desired result or draw the imagined successful scene. It was not a great jump to believe that the things humans could not control, but which happened anyway, were controlled by even more powerful, but unseen, humans. These became the spirits or gods. Indeed the earliest of these super humans were very human in that they had families and exhibited all the characteristics of normal humans such as anger, revenge, love, and ambition. Truly, the gods were conceived in the image of humans as is clear in Greek mythology.

As noted by Boyer, "If you live in a large enough group, there will probably be some people who seem better skilled at producing convincing messages from the counterintuitive agents [surrounding you]. These people will probably be considered as having some special internal quality that makes them different from the rest of the group. They will also end up by taking on a special role in ritual performances.... It is also very likely that they will form a sort of guild with attendant political goals."[10]

The people who could tap the power of the gods were, for that reason, very powerful members of the community. They were the medicine men and witchdoctors. They also evolved along with the society in which they lived.

As Frazer commented from his studies of culture in Africa:

> *... here the evidence for the evolution of the chief out of the magician, and especially out of the rainmaker, is comparatively plentiful. From simple magician to chief and on to king or queen, the role of conduit to the gods gave great secular power to the chosen individuals. Their commands, formulated from their own human desires, were given with all the awesome majesty of the gods. We have more or less passed the stage [in the early days of the 19th Century] of the absolute monarchs who had that second-hand authority but the priestly caste still retains the same power over a great mass of the people. Their special raiment, ceremonies and incantations to their particular god betrays their origin as magicians and witch-doctors but their authority is increasingly being contested as the transparent human base for their edicts conflicts with the real living needs of their subjects.*[11]
>
> *Once scientific investigation reveals, as it has done, the natural evolutionary origin of religion and its gods and its role in society as well as its confinement to our brain activity, the veil of mystery has parted. The "agnostics" can now make up their minds. God exists but only as a product of the evolving mind.*
>
> *Far from science and religion being separate magisteria they are, in fact, separate aspects of the one human endeavor to control the world in which we find ourselves. The idealist path of belief in the supernatural led through magic to religion and God and a dead end of endlessly interpreting and re-interpreting words to adjust to the changing demands of society. The materialist path led from experience and testing of the natural world through science to unending understanding.*[12]

I quote this source because it comes close to my view, which is that on occasion and within some small groups, a unique individual—perhaps an eccentric, an epileptic, or a hallucinating one (all about 1/1,000 chance in any individual)—became identified or identified himself with the explanation of the mysterious as a mystic. Thus was born the shaman who had widespread recognition in all cultural studies.

The identifying of the soul with breath is found in many places and times—in Tasmania, North America, and in Roman times, as well as in Semetic and Indo-European areas. Honoring the dead—animal and man—reflected the idea that the departed had gone on a type of journey and needed both ceremony and goods to acknowledge their departure and to support them either on their return or during their journey.

Over thousands of years and as the groups expanded in number and association, these ceremonies became more both stylized and more imbedded in the group consciousness. The ideas lasted for many more thousands of years and are seen in the burial ceremonies of Egypt and Mesopotamia. At Uruk in Iraq, the burial rites of the King involved his consort and many hundreds of courtiers, as well as animals—all deemed necessary for a pleasant afterlife journey.

All primitive societies seem to have this view—that the sky is the seat of forces, often personified as mainly similar to themselves, who oversee the affairs of the world. Contact with these forces was attempted via a variety of acts and rituals. These were often accompanied by (before full language had developed), mouth music, drumming and dancing. Rites, such as those undertaken among the Australian bushmen, of which there are photographs in Joseph Campbell's folio book *Historical Atlas of World Mythology:* Volume 1, Part 1, shows that attempts to contact the gods have been carried out for many thousands of years.

My selection of Australian aboriginal people to reference aspects of primitive man stems from the fact that these are true aboriginals both in the sense that they were the first to successfully make the journey out of Africa and that their descendents were the first who were rather unaffected by the spread of 'civilization.' The first ethnographers visited them in the late 1800s. Thus, I suppose that the early ethnographers were closer to a true 'primitive' than many others. A similar scenario is also painted by others who visited isolated islands and areas in the late 1800s. Now, excepting perhaps some remote, isolated tribes in the New Guinea interior or in the Amazon forests, and the miniature dwarf people discovered recently on Flores in Indonesia, there are no such people left in the world.

Many tribes and groups had secret ways open only to specific people. Shying away from close relationships with these ways helped to develop the concept of the 'sacred.'

The concept of the "sacred" refers to the way in which tribal mysteries of communicating with the Gods were arranged and hidden from the general view. In some areas, markings or paintings are considered sacred. In one instance, cave paintings in northern Australia's Arnhem Land area, made some 40,000 years ago, have been independently copied with fidelity by tribal members since they were originally executed. The paintings are considered sacred, as was their fidelity. That the copies of the cave art were all made from memory is astounding. This is an example of the transmission of ideas from generation to generation through what is now called a "meme," of which there will be more later.

Among the inferences made by all people was that of a higher mystery or a god—often an invisible presence of someone similar to one's self but with monumental powers. A recent publication asks:

> *"How, without any physical reality on which it could be based, have those images of God or gods taken hold in the human brain?*[13]

The scientific groundwork for an answer to that question was laid in 1890 when Sir J. G. Frazer published the results of his anthropological study of magic and religion in his book *The Golden Bough.* [14]With an overwhelming collection of data, Frazer showed that the idea of God had an evolutionary history. It started with the earliest human beings attempting to control their environment through magic. If you want rain, then splash water around. If you want success in the hunt, then dance the desired result or draw the imagined successful scene. It was not a great jump to believe that the things humans could not control, but which happened anyway, were controlled by even more powerful, but unseen, humans. These became the spirits, or gods. Indeed the earliest of these super humans were very human in that they had families and exhibited all the characteristics of normal humans such as anger, revenge, love and ambition. Truly, the gods were conceived in the image of humans as is clear in Greek mythology.

As noted by Boyer, "*If you live in a large enough group, there will probably be some people who seem better skilled at producing convincing messages from the counterintuitive agents [surrounding you]. These people will probably be considered as having some special internal quality that makes them different from the rest of the group. They will also end up taking on a special role in ritual performances.... It is also very likely that they will form a sort of guild with attendant political goals.*"[15]

The people who could tap the power of the gods were, for that reason, very powerful members of the community. They were the medicine men and witchdoctors. They also evolved along with the society in which they lived.

Magic and religion, or belief, are found all over the world but the shamans claimed particular abilities such as 'mastery over fire,' 'magical flight' and 'shape shifting,' where the shaman might seem to adopt the shape and manners of certain beasts. A shaman may be called a magician, but not all magicians are shamans—a shaman specializes in a trance during which his anima or soul leaves his body and ascends to the sky, or to the underworld that is the opposite of the sky.

As Eliade explains, 'shamans are of the 'elect' and are respected in their tribes or groups. Principally identified with the denizens of the Arctic, Siberia, and Central Asia who were hunter-gatherers or herdsmen and often migratory, shamans were the principal religious leaders. Most tribes revered a celestial Great God often named "Sky" or "Heaven." Even when such names were not used, it appears that deities with names like 'high,' 'lofty,' and 'luminous' are used. The Yakut tribe of Siberia call the celestial god "Lord Father Chief of the World," the Tatars "White Light," the Turko-Tatars call him "Chief," "Master," "Lord," and "Father." The only great god after God of the Sky or God of the Atmosphere is the "Lord of the Underworld"—Erlik Kahn.

Shamans and their trances were common worldwide.[16] They are found among the Apache Indians of the U.S. southwest; in Norse myths where Odin suffered on the World Tree so as to be able to raise the dead, fly, shape-shift and prophesy the future; among the Ogala Sioux, where Black Elk induced visions under a tree (the symbol of a cosmic pillar and of a connection to the sky); in shamanistic actions in the Asian sub-continent (Indonesia, Borneo, and the Celebes) where the Rice Mother was glorified; and in the South American jungles and highlands. These practices attest to the longevity of ancient customs and to ancient and common use of concepts about religion. After his séance, the shaman returns to the world of humans both feared and respected as healer, prophet and sage—but he is always apart from his fellows.[17] The report states, "The occurrence of ecstatic religious experience in patients with epilepsy, although controversial, is well documented ... Religious delusions are also commonly observed in the psychoses of epilepsy, occurring both between and immediately following a bout of seizures."

The world of the primitive was a narrow one. People always thought that where they were was the center of the universe. The centrality of the world with one at its center is widely noted in, for example, the Hindu Rig Veda (X, 149), which says the world grew from a point; and in Hebrew tradition, which has the center of the earth at its navel—Zion or Jerusalem. Centrality and a sacred space are also seen in Bali, in New Guinea, and in Algonquin lodges that signify the world. Mercia Eliade, in his book, *The Sacred and the Profane,*[18] states that a similar conception applies to villages and towns in the ancient German and Italian areas, where the *mundus,* or circular wall, was divided into four parts with a sacred space at the center. Both Eliade and Joseph Campbell note the awe that descends upon one on entering a "sacred" space be it church, cool forest glade, or the 20-storey atrium of a new building.

Additionally, the concept of the *axis mundi,* the center of the world, exists in shamanistic and other primitive societies. Sometimes it is a pole, a tree, or a place open to the sky at the center and is documented in the most primitive of societies—the *Kauwa-auwa* pole of the Australian Achilpa tribe is an example, as is the *tepee* of the North American Plains Indian. The Norse legend of the *Yggdrasil tree* represents another, as does Jacob's Ladder (Genesis 28:12). The early yearning for "contact" with the sky carries on into many other traditions. Cosmic representation is found in the very structure of the habitation and temple as it does in Ziggurats and Cathedrals where there is an obvious relation to a God on high. This upward-centered interest derives from the mystery of the wheeling stars above and seems to be both universal and the origin of many religions.

With the shaman came rituals to affect or reinforce the wizardry. Some shamans developed rituals associated with animals. The art of the French caves shows dressed shamans and numerous animals—the food of the group. Primitive dance, such as those described in, and shown photographically, in the series by Joseph Campbell,[19] as well as songs and dances, as related by Radciffe-Brown among the Andaman Islanders, were also used.

Noting that there was a slow change in the fabric of the stories told and, presumably, in the way in which information was given to the tribe over time, Radcliffe-Brown wrote about the local shamans in *The Andaman Islanders ...*

> "*... it was mentioned that there are certain individuals, known as oko-jumu in the North Andaman and oko-paiad in the South, who are believed to have special knowledge as to the spirits and as to the magical efficacy of remedies for sickness. It*

> *is these oko-jumu also who are the authorities on the legendary lore of the Andamanese. In the case of magical remedies there is a certain common stock of beliefs as to the efficacy to be attributed to different substances, such as leaves of different plants, and on the basis of these beliefs the oko-jumu elaborates the remedies that he uses in particular cases. Each oko-jumu, however, prides himself on being, to some extent, original. An example of this has been already mentioned. When a great storm arose an oko-jumu of one of the Northern tribes succeeded in stopping it (in the belief of the natives) by placing a piece of the crushed stem of the Anadendron creeper under a particular stone in the sea. On a later occasion, another storm arose, and the successor of the first-mentioned oko-jumu was appealed to that he might exert his powers. He did not simply imitate his predecessor, but he placed a piece of crushed bark and twigs of the Ficus laccifera in the sea under a different stone. In very much the same way there is a common stock of beliefs as to the events that took place in the time of the ancestors, but each oko-jumu builds up on this basis his own particular set of legends, so that it is rarely that two of them tell the same story in the same way. An oko-jumu may obtain for himself a reputation by relating legends of the ancestors in a vivid and amusing way. Such a man would be able to invent new stories by combining in his own way some of the traditional incidents. The desire on the part of each oko-jumu to be original and so to enhance his own reputation is a fertile source of variation in the legends."*[20]

This lack of traditional form, which is a very important characteristic of the Andaman mythology, may be compared with their lack of traditional songs. Just as every man composes his own songs, so, within certain limits, every *oko-jumu* relates in his own way the legends of his tribe. But, whereas, every man is a composer of songs, only a certain number are regarded as having authority to speak on the legends. So, it is in most shamanistic groups.

Underlying the legends of any tribe there are a certain number of beliefs or representations with which every native is familiar. It is on the basis of these that the *oko-jumu* elaborates his own doctrine, if we may call it so, which he hands on to his followers, who in turn may become *oko-jumu* and produce further slight modifications of their own. Thus, the legends are continually being changed, though in any one generation the changes introduced are slight, and it would take a long time for important changes in belief to be brought about. Radcliffe-Brown gives evidence, however, that a succession of leading men in the *A-Pučikwar* tribe have succeeded in introducing a new doctrine regarding the weather. This makes *Bilik* the name of a class of beings instead of the name of a single being, and that this doctrine, while it has not entirely ousted the former beliefs, has yet succeeded in gaining currency not only in the *A-Pučikwar* tribe, but also in the *Aka-Ko̲l* and *O̲ko̲-Juwo̲i* tribes.

Shamans also put an emphasis on rejuvenation among those living close to areas of heavy vegetation, the rejuvenation that was to be seen regularly in the growth of vegetation and the fruition of the plants. But they also noticed that rejuvenation involved dying so that sacrifice and death was allied to rebirth. Among some African tribes death was a precursor of rejuvenation, thus ritual killing came about with the leading tribal man, or chief, being put to death when his health failed (if he is sick then the whole tribe will get sick) or when an appropriate number of days or other time-measures had passed.

An entire religious scheme grew up around these simple ideas—the cults of the dying and resurrected god found around the agricultural world and even in the Pacific Islands. Animism was also a generally conceived method of strengthening the shaman. The *Yakuts* of Siberia used to believe that every shaman or wizard keeps his soul incarnate in an animal, invisible to the world; among the *Fan tribe of Gabon* every wizard was thought to have become blood brother to a ferocious animal and therefore to have deposited his soul outside himself and become invulnerable.[21]

In the shaman society one saw the shaman go into a trance and then return, as if he had died and then returned from what was often described as a journey. In that, dead bodies were viewed as a spiritual departure with a return. This was followed by specific doctrines about the treatment of the dead and the need to provide for their journey and possible return to the world of the living. Burial rituals were begun complete with grave goods to nourish the departed.

Exclusivity of beliefs, differentiation between in-and-out groups and sectarian violence between in- and out-groups followed as tribes encroached on the territories of others. Because religion was rich in inferences and thus of great value for tribal cohesion, it spread quickly over the area of human occupation and because God or the shaman was supposed to have all the information needed to make correct judgments, the shaman or it (He or She) was always turned to for defining morality. In addition, the shaman's God was often associated with the sun, the moon and the stars (or planets), and their movements and arrangements as other-worldly indicators of specific human situations and the hoped-for or predicted likely regular future. Thus, there came about a concentration on the heavens and their use in indicating the change of seasons. A visit to Stonehenge, to Newgrange, in Ireland, or to Inca and the Indian temples will reveal the importance given in the earliest days to timekeeping.

There may be many ways to explain the "morphing" of shamans into kings or priests, excepting that shamans persisted among the nomads until the late 19th Century. The head-man, likely a rainmaker, co-opted the leadership of the tribe—after all he was the one who knew the future. He adopted the role of shaman and King. Shamans, though, have almost ceased to exist, except in the far reaches of contemporary societies, (that is if we ignore the fulminators in Islam and Christianity, who today attract large audiences in both person and electronically). The clue to the wane of shamanism was the worldwide shift from hunter-gatherer to agriculturalist in the areas better suited to growing foods. In Africa, this would indicate a date of about 15,000 BC. Agriculture spread slowly to fertile lands as the knowledge of it spread. The late Joseph Campbell provides one of the best explanations of how the clash between shaman and priest came about and was ultimately won by the priest in agricultural areas. He relates the clash between the hunter shamans and the agriculturalist priests that occurred among the Apache Indians of New Mexico, as told in their creation myth, saying that it illustrates the capitulation of the religiosity represented by the shaman to the more structured religion of the priest.

In this long myth it appears that the gods, called *Hactcin,* and led by the powerful *Black Hactcin,* asked the shamans to bring back an extinguished sun,[22] but they failed after trying their many wiles, chants, and supplications. In the face of this failure of their shamans, the Black *Hactcin* selected many shamans (24 total) and made them into dolls of various colors and types. These dolls are still used by the Apache in their dances. The shamans were publicly discredited in their Paleolithic type practices and given a minor place in the liturgical structure of the group-oriented and rather more complex organization of a seed-planting economy. This change represents what happened all over the agricultural world—a discrediting of the individualistic and unpredictable force of the individual in favor of a socially anointed priesthood of the non-nomadic agricultural society. All over the world, this new agriculturally based society required a regimentation ordained by the growing cycle and the need for tending the crops that recognized death and rejuvenation.

Campbell says, and I have no doubt that he is correct, "The highest concern of all the mythologies, ceremonials, ethical systems, and social organization of agricultural based societies has been that of suppressing the manifestations of individualism. And this has been generally achieved by compelling or persuading people to identify themselves, not with their own interests, intuitions and modes of experience, but with the archetypes of behavior and systems of sentiment developed and maintained in the public domain. The emphasis of the planting societies is on the group, that of the hunters and nomads on the individual." This had great implications for the development and practices of religion—it became more demanding of adherents.

Eliade says, "Given the economic, social, and religious parallels between the ancient indo-European peoples and the ancient Proto-Turks (Turko-Tatar), we must determine to what extent the various historical Indo-European peoples still preserve shamanic survivals comparable to Turko-Tatar shamanism." He continues, "Nothing justifies the supposition that during the hundreds of thousands of years that preceded the earliest Stone Age, humanity did not have a religious life as intense and various as in the succeeding periods. It is almost certain that a part of prelithic humanity's magico-religious beliefs were preserved in later religious conceptions and mythologies."

The most important difference between the primitive shamanistic societies—in general the societies of the hunter-gatherers—and the Indo-Europeans, whose invasions from the east came to dominate and overthrow the earlier societal ideas and impose patriarchy, was matriarchy.

This preservation of old ideas and concepts of shamanism is clearly seen in the ziggurat, whose seven levels relate to the seven visible planets. The basic idea of these structures was to elevate the shaman or priest toward God. Ziggurats were made as early as the 6th millennium BCE and continued to be built in Mesopotamia until about 300 BCE. The temple at Babylon is perhaps the best known to us as one of the "Seven Wonders of the World." However, ziggurats were also seen in India, in China, and in Central North America where religious functions were also performed, some of a sacrificial nature.

While an original or first shaman may have been self-selected, and that the shaman begins his new, true life by a separation and a spiritual crisis that is, as Eliade says, "not lacking in tragic greatness and in beauty." Most shamans are recruited through hereditary transmission of the profession or by a spontaneous "call." However selected, a shaman is not recognized as such until he has received teaching in the ecstatic—dreams, trances, etc—and in the traditional—names, techniques, mythology and clan genealogy, functions of the spirits and secret language. In some areas, Lapland for example, the shaman must also be accepted by the family.

In regions other than Siberia, the medicine men, or shamans, are hereditary positions. Among the Zulus and Bechuana of South Africa, they are also hereditary, as they are in the southern Sudan, among the tribes of Malaysia, the Batak, the people of Sumatra, the Dyak, among the sorcerers of the New Hebrides, in Guianan tribes, and in many Amazon tribes as well. Among Rocky Mountain tribes in North America, shamanistic powers may be inherited, but the transmission of powers is always through an ecstatic experience. Among the Plateau tribes of North America—Thompson, Shuswap, Okanagan, Nez Perce and Kalmath—the medicine man status is often hereditary as well.

The rites of the shaman often involve passage from one cosmic region to another—from earth to sky or from earth to the underworld. The three cosmic regions (up-down and earth-underworld) are linked together by a cosmic axis or hole in the universe that is available only to the shaman. The axis passes through this opening, often the opening in the roof of a yurt or tepee. It is through this opening that the soul of the shaman 'flies' to the gods.

The sky is seen as a tent. The Milky Way is the seam that opens when the gods wish to see the earth, and the stars are holes, the windows of the world, through which ventilation for the celestial spheres, sometimes seven and sometimes nine, takes place. In the middle of the sky shines the Pole star, holding the celestial tent like a stake. The Samoyed call it "Sky Nail," and others the "Nail Star." That terminology extends to the Lapps, the Finns, and the Estonians, as well as throughout the Siberian area. The central pillar is a characteristic element in the dwellings of many of the people of North America.

The world pillar is often represented within the house or apart from it. Charlemagne destroyed such a pillar in Germany in 772.

The symbolism of the World Pillar is also seen within more developed cultures—Egypt, India, China, Greece, and Mesopotamia. The associated 'high place', symbolized by the Cosmic Mountain, is evident in the ziggurats and by the concept of Mount Meru in Hindu and Buddhist mythology. Above the mountain shines the pole star. The world pillar is also evident in the myth of Jacob's Ladder and in the Christian myth of Golgotha, where Adam is buried and where the blood of Jesus falls on Adam's skull and redeems him.

So, the concept of the World Tree, the *axis mundi*, has a long history expressing the sacredness of the world, its fertility and fecundity and absolute reality and immortality. Thus, the World Tree also becomes the Tree of Life and Immortality and it is enriched by numerous associated symbols—woman, wellspring, animals, fruit, a reservoir of life and destiny, and the Christian cross.

Now one supposes that such men, as shamans, in their more lucid moments, realized that having or inducing trances which the rest of the tribe saw as 'otherworldly experiences,' was worth more than just respect. Being human and having a self-saving attitude, the shamans generally and gradually expanded their actions by stating that they flew to other parts of the sky to commune with the Sky God or the Sun God. The shaman became a medicine man and a familiar with the Gods. His sayings and healings were closely attended to and revered—when the healing did not work the shaman often blamed other factors.

Creation stories or myths often involve water.[23] "Water, thou art the source of all things and of all existence," says an Indian text summarizing a Vedic work whose priests used to pray, "May the water bring us well being." In the mythology of the American Indians, the hieroglyphic for water is always associated with moon images, which also apply to the symbolism of fertility and to every level of nature. In the Puranic tradition of India, Vishnu floats on the primeval waters and from his navel arises the lotus (representing a tree) from whose center Brahma is born. In other versions, some recalling certain North American myths, Vishnu, in his third reincarnation as a boar, dives into the waters and brings up the earth from the abyss.

The Babylonian creation story also tells of a watery chaos of "apsu" and "tiamat," the former personifies fresh water on which the earth was to float; the second (tiamat) was salty and bitter, inhabited by monsters, among whom was Leviathan, noted in the Bible. The water story, a creation poem often studied today, is written in the Enuma Elish. Underlying these types of belief is the fundamental idea that life and reality is concentrated in one cosmic substance from which all living forms proceed. Water animals, particularly fish and sea monsters, become emblems of the sacred because they stand for absolute reality concentrated in water.

In the Lake Baikal area of Russia, the Buriats (a tribe of Mongols) tell their story of the Great Spirit moving over the waters and commanding a water-bird to dive to the depths and bring back "earth, black soil, in your beak and red clay in your feet," so this became the earth. A similar tale or myth of creation of the earth from diving birds is also found in North America among the Thompson River Indians and the Cree Indians of Georgia and Alabama, some 3,000 miles away.

Water comes to be regarded as a healing material and a force of life. In the Apocalypse, the two symbols are side by side—"And he showed me a river of water of life, clear as crystal, proceeding from the throne of God and of the Lamb ... and on both sides of the river was the tree of life." The Iranian water divinity is called, "the holy one who multiplies flocks ... goods ... riches ... land ... etc." Ablution purifies and is often needed for man to prepare his entry into the realm of the sacred—there are ablutions needed before going into temples and before sacrifices. The ceremony of the sacred bath was generally performed in the cults of the Great Goddess of fertility and agriculture. Many Greek rituals involved baths, as did some rituals of Cretan and German tribes. Catholics dipped a statue of Mary into water to end droughts and this went on (despite ecclesiastical opposition), into the twentieth century. Ultimately, the ceremony of Baptism is derived from this background.

The world was, however, changing slowly. From hunter-gatherers and herders, humans invented agriculture, probably first in Africa where humans had discovered that certain plants and fruits could be eaten safely. The beginning of proper agriculture came through searching for seeds that had blown away or fallen onto the ground or were ripening on their stalks. From the original grasses, random genetic change produced a type of related grass that dropped its seeds onto the ground and were too heavy to be blown about easily. This improved human use and, consequently, another genetic change took place that resulted in even heavier seeds that tended to remain longer on the stalk when ripe. This was primitive barley and it was used by the inhabitants of northern Israel about 7,000 years BCE. From there, the cultivation of barley, first ploughing with sticks and later with beasts, became widespread.

The spread of agriculture was slow as it extended haltingly into the forests and plains of the Middle East and all of Europe, as can be seen from the map below. It took almost 3,000 years for agriculture to spread from the Middle East to Britain. During the transition from a nomadic and hunter-gatherer life where the clear importance of the male is obvious in the hunt, the new life based on agriculture accentuated the female role as more important. She participated and was predominant in the new way of life, in the planting and reaping of crops, and in caring for the small animals that began to surround the village or encampments. She is seen as a nourisher of life and as a helpmate to the earth. Thus developed the generalized cult of the Great Mother. As agriculture spread, so did the cult of the Great Mother.

One authority[24] states, "*There is no evidence in all of Old Europe of a patriarchal chieftenate of the Indo-European type [where the male was supreme]. No male royal tombs, no residences on hills or hill forts have been found and … the distribution of wealth in grave goods speaks of an economic egalitarianism.*"

It is at this time in the human journey that numerous clay figurines are found, such as the Venus of Lussel, the Venus of Lespugue and other generalized Great Goddess or Great Mother figures. Various symbols associated with her also began to appear. She is sometimes shown with a bull-headed child, the bull being reflective of the Moon that dies in the sky and is resurrected three days later. Her main symbols are Mirror, Throne of Wisdom, Gate, and Morning and Evening Star. Compare these with the words associated and applied to the Virgin Mary—Holy Mother of God, Mirror of Justice, Seat of Wisdom, Gate of Heaven, Morning Star, and House of God, among others.

Later, during the time that Campbell calls High Neolithic (4,500–3,500 BCE), motifs associated with the Great Mother spread. Designs with the swastika and Star were found in pottery called Halaf Ware and Samarra Ware dating to about 4,000 BCE. Other pottery with similar designs were found at the city of Ur, from which Father Abram and his wife Sari departed (Genesis 11.31)

This period is also associated with the names Ishtar and Tammuz, Venus and Adonis, Isis and Osiris, whose stories are of particular interest. For example in AD 431, at Ephesus the Virgin Mary was declared to be "the Godbearer." But this was at the greatest temple of the goddess Artemis, sculpted with a multitude of breasts. There is a Hindu version of her story and a more modern commentary relates that Artemis (Diana) was the Mother without a spouse, the original mother; all are my children.

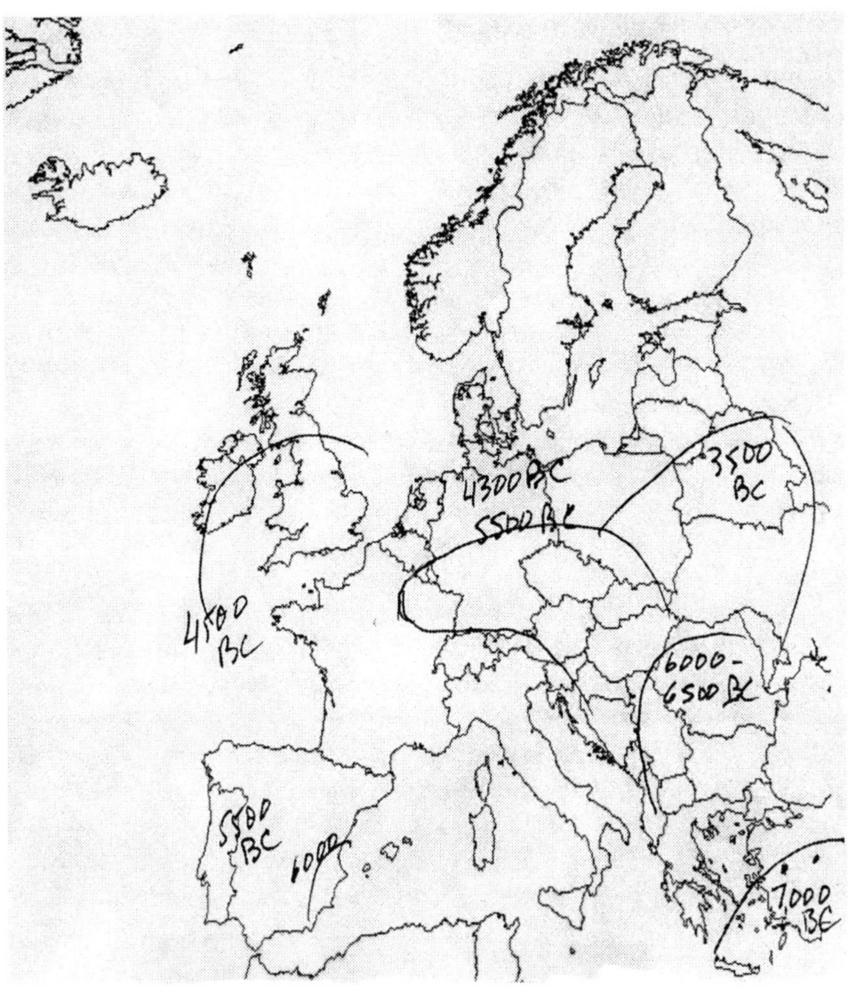

APPROXIMATE DATES FOR SPREAD OF

AGRICULTURE IN EUROPE

BASED ON MARJITA GIMBUTAS "THE CIVILIZATION OF THE GODDESS"
Harper Collins, San Francisco, 1991

The Priest and King in Religion

Agriculture developed, probably in Africa, and spread with varying success to the Middle East around 10,000 BC. From there, it spread or more likely was independently developed. By 10,000 BC, the Atlantic and Pacific coasts of Europe and Asia saw agricultural development. In the Indus Valley and on the Chinese river banks agricultural invention is now established. In many of these areas shamanistic practices retreated in the face of the pressures brought by the time oriented demands of agriculture. Further development in the relationship of shaman, priest and King occurred in the period of about 3,500 to 2,500 BC and that gave rise in the central areas to kingship, priesthood, the temple, the wheel, mathematics record keeping and (unhappily) taxation. These findings and changes spread rapidly once again to the two coasts through invention but also by traders. Nonetheless, it was in the Sumerian mud garden, known as Uruk, that both ritual marriage at the top of the new temple to the Gods on high, the Ziggurat, and the development of an ordered priestly class was invented.

Agriculture provided the priests and merchants of Sumer with free time that they used to invent mathematics. They became adept in its use. They began to plot the movements of the heavens and to identify specific stars, planets, and constellations. Over a period of many years, the priests were able to gradually convince the people that the stars somehow governed in a mystical way the life, thought, and actions of men on earth. The whole city was seen to be a microcosm of the heavens and the link between man and the governing heavens was the priesthood, the only ones who understood the heavens. This powerful religious notion—that the heavens contained the answers to worldly problems—lived on for many centuries into Greece, Rome, and the early Christian sects—and in the zodiac, still printed in today's newspapers. The pivotal center of the universe and of the city was, to the Sumerians, the Ziggurat and the priests controlled a calendar governing the city's life. All of these developments were captured in the newly invented writing. Nor did the King escape the attentions of the priesthood.

This wonderful assembly of priestly ideas—kingship, priesthood, mathematics, and calendarical astronomy—first reached the Nile from Sumer to inspire the First Dynasty, then spread to Crete, to the Indus Valley by 2,600 BCE, to Shang China by about 1,600 BCE (and perhaps, say some, to Middle America and the Peruvian coast about 700 BCE). The Ziggurat also marched around the world with this religious idea and it is seen in India, China, and in Central America, always carrying with it the idea of a God on high.

An accord of heavenly, earthly, and individual affairs is imagined in this strongly growing religiosity. The priests ensured that his virgin priestess would accompany and serve the dying King in death. She would be his bride on the planet Venus. Not only would those two die, but so would many, many others at the same time—acolytes and servants. As Joseph Campbell says, "What a marvelous game—and what a scam to secure the continuity and powers of the priests!"

The full power of the priest and the King to bind the society together through religion and sacrifice to the rejuvenation of crops is no more clearly seen than in the recorded practices of the Aztecs of ancient Mexico. The Jesuit, Acosta, [25]in the 1600s AD describes primitive religious rites that were then still carried on:

> "*They took a captive such as they thought good; and afore they did sacrifice him unto their idols, they gave him the name of the idol, to whom he should be sacrificed, and appareled him with the same ornaments like their idol, saying that he did represent the same idol. And during the time that this representation lasted, which was for a year in some feasts, in others six months, and in others less. They reverenced and worshiped him in the same manner as the proper idol; and in the meantime he did eat, drink and was merry.... The feast being come and he grown fat, they kicked [*KILLED*] him, opened him, and ate him, making a solemn sacrifice of him.*"[26]

The Franciscan monk, Fra. Sahagun, states that a young woman was annually sacrificed in the character of the God of Gods at the great Mexican festival called Toxcat. This was also after having been maintained for a year and worshiped as that great deity. According to the Aztec calendar, this sacrifice took place within a few days of what would be Christian or Pagan Easter—the first day of the Aztec fifth month or between the 23rd or 27th of April. This feast and sacrifice was related to the annual reverence of the Corn, the staple food of the masses. Frazer in, Chapter 59, *The Golden Bough*, gives the rather grisly description of the actual ceremony and sacrifice in detail. Such a sacrifice coming at that time leads one to suppose, as we shall see later, that many other sacrificial actions were taken in other places at about that same time.

So, it comes about, all over the world and at different times in history that the King and the Priest are symbiotically joined in ritual. Both survive, one as part of an order, the other through his progeny. And so it was, until recently. Thus was demonstrated the power of religion in the agriculturally based systems of life—no longer viable in the modern age. Perhaps the general repugnance toward religions based upon sacrifice indicates why church attendance seems to decline. Information about current church attendance (all churches) indicates that it declines with the degree of industrialization of the society.[27]

Yet, the old ways of the animists, the sorcerers, and the regenerative powers in religion lived on far beyond the times of early humans. It is from that background that the ancient cults of Astarte, relying on sexual congress and on human sacrifice to express the unity of humans and regeneration, were formed.

The old religions also involved sacrifice, sometimes human and sometimes of living animals that represented the human. The origin of the practice is lost and can only be developed through mythical beings or stories. One such story that involves many elements seen in Christian religion is that of Dionysus, God of fertility and nature, also related to trees, vines and wine. He was probably originally a Thracian god of the Balkans and southeast Europe. Here are two notes and a story that blends fertility, orgiastic rites, resurrection and trees (the world tree theme noted before). One is from Middle Europe and Greece; the other is from Aztec America. Both deal with regeneration.

Dionysus

> The most characteristic manifestation of Dionysus was the vine with its clusters of grapes; he was also a god of trees in general. Thus, we are told that almost all the Greeks sacrificed to "Dionysus of the tree." In Boeotia (in central Greece), one of his titles was "Dionysus in the tree." His image was often merely an upright post, without arms, but draped in a mantle, with a bearded mask to represent the head, and with leafy boughs projecting from the head or body to show the nature of the deity. Amongst the trees particularly sacred to him, in addition to the vine, was the pine-tree. The Delphic oracle commanded the Corinthians to worship a particular pine-tree "equally with the god," so they made two images of Dionysus out of it, with red faces and gilt bodies. In art, the god and/or his worshippers, commonly carry a wand, tipped with a pinecone.
>
> Further, there are indications, few but significant, that Dionysus was conceived as a deity of agriculture and the corn. He is spoken of as himself doing the work of a husbandman. He is reported to have been the first to yoke oxen to the plough, which before had been dragged by hand alone; and some people found in this tradition the clue to the bovine shape in which, as we shall see, the god was often supposed to present himself to his worshippers. Thus, guiding the ploughshare and scattering the seed as he went, Dionysus is said to have eased the labor of the husbandman.

Like other gods of vegetation, Dionysus was believed to have died a violent death, and to have been torn apart when hiding in the aspect of a bull. But he was brought to life again; and his sufferings, death, and resurrection were enacted in his sacred rites.

According to some, the severed limbs of Dionysus were pieced together, at the command of Zeus, by Apollo, who buried them on Parnassus. The grave of Dionysus was shown in the Delphic temple beside a golden statue of Apollo. However, according to another account, it is simply said that shortly after his burial he rose from the dead and ascended up to heaven.

Turning from the myth to the ritual, we find that the Cretans celebrated a biennial festival at which the passion of Dionysus was represented in every detail. All that he had done or suffered in his last moments was enacted before the eyes of his worshippers, who tore a live bull to pieces with their teeth and roamed the woods with frantic shouts. In front of them was carried a casket that was supposed to contain the sacred heart of Dionysus, and to the wild music of flutes and cymbals they mimicked the rattles by which the infant god had been lured to his doom. Where the resurrection formed part of the myth, it also was acted at the rites. It even appears that a general doctrine of resurrection, or at least of immortality, was inculcated on the worshippers; for Plutarch, writing to console his wife on the death of their infant daughter, comforts her with the thought of the immortality of the soul as taught by tradition and revealed in the mysteries of Dionysus.

The Bacchanals of Thrace wore horns in imitation of their god. According to the myth, it was in the shape of a bull that he was torn to pieces by the Titans; and the Cretans, when they reenacted the sufferings and death of Dionysus and tore a live bull to pieces with their teeth. Indeed, the rending and devouring of live bulls and calves appears to have been a regular feature of the Dionysian rites. When we consider the practice of portraying the god as a bull or with some of the features of the animal, the belief that he appeared in bull form to his worshippers at the sacred rites, and the legend that in bull form he had been torn in pieces: we cannot doubt that in rending and devouring a live bull at his festival the worshippers of Dionysus believed themselves to be killing the god, eating his flesh, and drinking his blood. Savages have practiced the custom of tearing in pieces the bodies of animals and of men and then devouring them raw as a religious rite in modern times. We need not therefore dismiss as a fable the testimony of antiquity to the observance of similar rites among the frenzied worshippers of Bacchus.

The custom of killing a god in animal form belongs to a very early stage of human culture, and is apt in later times to be misunderstood. The advance of thought tends to strip the old animal and plant gods of their bestial and vegetable husk, and to leave their human attributes (which are always the kernel of the conception) as the final and sole residuum. In other words, animal and plant gods tend to become purely anthropomorphic. When they have become wholly or nearly so, the animals and plants, which were at first the deities themselves, still retain a vague and ill-understood connection with the anthropomorphic gods who developed out of them. Various stories have been invented to explain the origin of the relationship between the deity and the animal or plant having been forgotten. These explanations may follow one of two lines, according as they are based on the habitual or on the exceptional treatment of the sacred animal or plant. The sacred animal was habitually spared, and only exceptionally slain; and accordingly the myth might be devised to explain either why it was spared or why it was killed. Devised for the former purpose, the myth would tell of some service rendered to the deity by the animal; devised for the latter purpose, the myth would tell of some injury inflicted by the animal on the god.

The reason given for sacrificing goats to Dionysus exemplifies a myth of the latter sort. They were sacrificed to him, it was said, because they injured the vine. Now the goat, as we have seen, was originally an embodiment of the god himself. But when the god had divested himself of his animal character and had become essentially anthropomorphic, the killing of the goat in his worship came to be regarded no longer as a slaying of the deity himself, but as a sacrifice offered to him. Furthermore, since some reason had to be assigned why the goat in particular should be sacrificed, it was alleged that this was a punishment inflicted on the goat for injuring the vine, the object of the god's especial care. Thus, we have the strange spectacle of a god being sacrificed to himself because he is his own enemy. Consequently, as the deity is supposed to partake of the victim offered to him, it follows that, when the victim is the god's old self, the god eats of his own flesh.

However, a tradition of human sacrifice may sometimes have been a mere misinterpretation of a sacrificial ritual in which an animal victim was treated as a human being. For example, at Tenedos (Rhodes) the newborn calf sacrificed to Dionysus was shod in buskins, and the mother cow was tended like a woman in childbed. In Rome, a she goat was sacrificed to Vedijovis as if it were a human victim. On the other hand it is equally possible, and perhaps more probable, that these curious rites were themselves mitigations of an older and ruder custom of sacrificing human beings. Consequently, the later pretence of treating the sacrificial victims as if they were human beings was merely part of a pious and merciful fraud, which palmed off on the deity less precious victims than living men and women. This interpretation is supported by many undisputable cases in which animals have been substituted for human victims.

Aztec Rites

Here, now, is a description, from *The Golden Bough* about the Aztec custom of sacrifice that was performed to ensure the corn crop in the coming season.

> At a great festival in September, which was preceded by a strict fast of seven days, they sanctified a young slave girl of twelve or thirteen years, the prettiest they could find, to represent the Maize Goddess, Chicomecohuatl[28]. They invested her with the ornaments of the goddess, putting a mitre on her head, maize-cobs round her neck and in her hands, and fastening a green feather upright on the crown of her head to imitate an ear of maize. This they did, we are told, in order to signify that the maize was almost ripe at the time of the festival, but because it was still tender, they chose a girl of tender years to play the part of the Maize Goddess. The whole long day they led the poor child in all her finery, with the green plume nodding on her head, from house to house dancing merrily to cheer people after the dullness and privations of the fast.
>
> In the evening, all the people assembled at the temple, the courts of which they lit up by a multitude of lanterns and candles. There they passed the night without sleeping, and at midnight, while the trumpets, flutes, and horns discoursed solemn music; a portable framework or palanquin was brought forth, bedecked with festoons of maize-cobs and peppers arid filled with seeds of all sorts. This the bearers set down at the door of the chamber in which the wooden image of the goddess stood. Now the chamber was adorned and wreathed, both outside and inside, with wreaths of maize-cobs, peppers, pumpkins, roses, and seeds of every kind, a wonder to behold; the whole floor was covered deep with these verdant offerings of the pious. When the music ceased, a solemn procession came forth of priests and dignitaries, with flaring lights and smoking censers, leading-in their midst the girl who played the part of the goddess. Then they made her mount the framework, where she stood upright on the maize and peppers and pumpkins with which it was strewed, her hands resting on two banisters to keep from falling. Then the priests swung the smoking censers round her; the music struck up again, and while it played, a great dignitary of the temple suddenly stepped up to her with a razor in his hand and adroitly shore off the green feathers she wore on her head, together with the hair in which it was fastened, snipping the locks off by the root.
>
> The feather and the hair he then presented to the wooden image of the goddess with great solemnity and elaborate ceremonies, weeping and giving her thanks for the fruits of the earth and the abundant crops which she had bestowed on the people that year; and as he wept and prayed, all the people, standing in the courts of the temple, wept and prayed with him. When that ceremony was over, the girl descended from the framework and was escorted to the place where she was to spend the rest of the night. But all the people

kept watch in the courts of the temple by the light of torches until break of day. The morning being come, and the courts of the temple being still crowded by the multitude, who would have deemed it sacrilege to quit the precincts, the priests again brought forth the damsel attired in the costume of the goddess, with the mitre on her 'head and the cobs of maize about her neck.' Again, she mounted the portable framework or palanquin and stood on it, supporting herself by her hands on the banisters. Then the elders of the temple lifted it off their shoulders, and while some swung burning censers and others played on instruments or sang, they carried it in procession through the great courtyard to the hall of the god Huitzilopochtli and then back to the chamber, here stood the wooden image of the Maize Goddess, whom the girl impersonated. There they caused the damsel to descend from the palanquin and to stand on the heaps of com and vegetables that had been spread in profusion on the floor of the sacred chamber. While she stood there all the elders and nobles came in a line, one behind the other, carrying saucers full of dry and clotted blood that they had drawn from their ears by way of penance during the seven days fast. One by one they squatted on their haunches before her, which was the equivalent of falling on their knees with us, and scraping the crust of blood from the saucer cast it down, before her as an offering in return for the benefits which she, as the embodiment of the Maize Goddess, had conferred upon them. When the men had thus humbly offered their blood to the human representative of the goddess, the women, forming a long line, did so likewise, each one of them dropping on her haunches before the girl and scraping her blood from the saucer. The ceremony lasted a long time, for great and small, young and old, all without exception had to pass before the incarnate deity and make their offering. When it was over, the people returned home with glad hearts to feast on flesh and viands of every sort as merrily, we are told, as good Christians at Easter partake of meat and other carnal mercies after the long abstinence of Lent. And when they had eaten. And drunk their fill. And rested after the night watch, they returned quite refreshed to the temple to see the end of the festival. And the end of the festival was this. The multitude being assembled, the priests solemnly incensed the girl who personated the goddess. Then they threw her on her back on the heap of corn and seeds, cut off her head, caught the gushing blood in a tub, and sprinkled the blood on the wooden image of the goddess, the walls of the chamber and the offerings of corn, peppers, pumpkins, seeds, and vegetables which covered the floor.

After that, they flayed the headless trunk, and one of the priests made swift to squeeze himself into the bloody skin. Having done so they clad him in the robes which the girl had worn; they put the mitre on his head, the necklace of golden maize-cobs about his neck, the maize cobs of gold and feathers in his hands; and thus arrayed they led him forth in public, all of them dancing to the beat of a drum, while he acted as fugleman, skipping and posturing at the head of the procession as briskly as he could be expected to do, encumbered as he was by the tight and clammy skin of the girl and her clothes, which must have been much too small for a grown man.

Killing the King

Themes of killing the king or leader are widespread in the past. A custom that originated many, many years before 300BCE concerned the ritual killing of the King of a tribe in the Upper Nile area. The practice ended with the spread of Greek humanism among the rulers. However, the ritual killing continued among remote African tribes. Among these were the Shilluk of the Sudan who continued the practice to about the time that the reports were recorded by Sir James G Frazer in about 1912. Priests, every seven years, or if the crops or the cattle did not prosper, determined that the King would be ritually killed by strangulation on a dark night. He was buried with a living Virgin at his side usually in the period just before the planting of the next crop.

Similar practices were carried out in Angola, Mozambique, Rhodesia, and India. In this latter case, the God-King had to sacrifice himself every 12 years according to signs seen in the stars. He sacrificed himself by cutting off parts of his flesh, finally cutting his throat and bleeding to death. The motif here is the death of the King/God.

Around 3500–2500 BCE the literate era dawns and calendars, priestcraft, royalty and a society ordered by the calculations of the heavens begins. The mystery of the planets begins to be seen in the way that the death of the King was treated. At the royal tombs of Ur, the King's death was accompanied by the deaths of all of the members of the court plus about 63 in the death pit and 25 with the Queen. In other tombs, the bodies of 68 women were found, all dressed in ceremonial robes.

This idea came from Mesopotamia and the region between the Caspian Sea and the Persian Gulf. It then spread into India and into the Dravidian cult; it also spread across Arabia and into East Africa.

Another level of sacrifice affected the peasants in the culture of tropical farming/gardening areas. In all of these areas, not only was the death of the King accompanied by the extinguishing of all tribal holy fires, but also the fires were later rekindled by a pubescent boy and a young virgin. When they had rekindled the sacred fire of the tribe, they were put to death by being buried alive. The lists of tribes wherein this rite was practiced many years ago are legion.

Among the hunting and gathering/gardening tribes, killing was the manner in which they celebrated the resurrection of crops from year to year. In one sense, the killing of game was a duty and it had ritual elements—the thanking of the animal before it was killed, and after, and the use of significant animals as totems or shrines or objects of veneration.

Among the gardening groups, harvesting was analogous to killing. From the earth came their life and to the earth, they returned both the dead matter left after use and the dead people who had lived on the plants it produced.

In New Guinea—7,000 miles from East Africa and the Sudan—at the time of the conclusion of puberty rites of many boys, a young girl is made to lie under a platform of heavy logs. In full view of the assemblage, each boy cohabits with the girl. As the last boy joins with her, the platform is collapsed and both die. They are immediately cut up, roasted and eaten. This rite imitates life and death in the plant world and is similar to such rites in Africa, India, and other places.

A continuum established, based on 5500–5400BCE in Middle East, then in the myths and rituals of planting tribes in East and South Africa and the Sudan, in Malabar, in Indonesia and Melanesia.

Compare all this with the Christian myth of the killed, buried, resurrected and eaten Jesus, whose ritual is the mystery of the altar, the blood and wine and the wheaten wafer.

Monotheism and Other Concepts

If we bring the time up to around 700 to 500 BCE, there begins a variety of themes that live on until today. The concept of monotheism, which was first seen in the West in Zarathustran religion in Iran, was rejuvenated in Judaism and adopted, with additions (the Trinity) by Christians. Some Jewish ideas were also adopted by Muslims.

There are also differences between most Asian religions and those of the West—with the Buddhist, Hindu, and Taoist religions related more to personal achievement and struggle to achieve a higher level of understanding, leading, perhaps, to a concept of unity and regeneration of soul or body. Human nature is not a subject of religious introspection in these areas, it is taken as a given and assumes that all are vulnerable to acting in kin-group-ways and in ways that contest outsiders. Attainment of nirvana or wholeness is the goal of those religions.

No serious thought was given by any of these religions to an abstract human nature—man responded to the will of the Gods and that was that.

Culturally successful religious concepts result from selective happenings that make some symbols or concepts more easily stored in the brain and transmitted than others. Human imagination, the unique ability of humans to discuss the idea of an object with others and have a common realization of what is under discussion, seems to interrelate with metaphysical principles so that supernatural concepts are developed. These supernatural concepts are exposed to the general cognitive capacities of humans for social interaction. Some of these concepts are connected to morality, strong group identity, ritual, and emotions and all have information needed for social interaction. Religious concepts also engender mental systems that deal with animacy (aliveness), social exchanges, morality, fear, and suspicion or caution about natural hazards and misfortune.

One can say that religion answers metaphysical questions, but it is also the case that religious thoughts are activated when people deal with concrete situations, such as a specific death, a crop gain or failure, a birth or a disease. Religion is thought to be about a transcendent God, but it is also about a range of agents such as ghouls, ghosts, spirits, ancestors, animals, etc in direct interaction with people. Religion is supposed to allay anxiety and it may for some, but for others, religion generates anxiety through vengeful ghosts, gods, or a world of spirits—the good and the vengeful may be about equal. Religion was thought to have been created at a certain time in history, but while the capacity for religiosity may have been with humans since symbolism was acquired, formal religions developed in all cultures at various times through various processes.

Religion is also thought to be about morality, but a sense of fairness was implicit in humans at the dawn of intelligence. The experience of living and of exchange applied and extended moral precepts to new situations. It is said that religion is about the salvation of the soul, but salvation is unheard of in many religions, though it is central to Christianity, Islam, and the doctrinal religions of Asia. In some other areas, the soul is taken by an animal when the human dies. Religion, it is claimed, creates social cohesion. I think this was important in early human history until recent times, but cohesion is often a seedbed for fission, as the Crusades, Indian wars, and the post-Reformation proliferation of sects and wars have shown in Christianity. This is less true in other religions, many of which have unchanged dogmas for millennia.

It now remains to show how humans may have carried the general concept of religion around the world and why some areas of the world have completely escaped mythology as we have come to know it today.

2

EVOLUTION, EVOLUTIONARY PSYCHOLOGY AND HUMAN NATURE

Evolution

So, what exactly is evolution? And why is it relevant to religiosity and to mythology? At the simplest level, evolution is change. Biological evolution is change in the properties of populations that last longer than an individual life. Evolutionary changes are those that are inherited through genes from one generation to the next. Biological evolution refers to a population level change.

Religiosity, the brain's ability to construct inferences involving the universal elements of religion, appears common to all societies and is changed and passed on both in the usual evolutionary manner, as noted at the beginning of this book, and through another evolutionary mechanism as well, *memes,*[29] which is noted below.

Two million species of plants and animals have already been discovered; and there are likely some 10 to 30 million yet to be discovered. (At least 13,000 new species were recently discovered in the ocean depths and others were discovered in both Indonesia and New Guinea.) All have a similar genetic make-up—the one shown by Crick and Watson (see APPENDIX A)—using DeoxyRiboNucleaicAcid, or DNA. The book, *The Double Helix*, shows how our genome is constructed—breathtakingly simple yet wonderfully complex. We are only now able to see its many complexities. Only four nucleotides, or DNA constituents, are involved: except that an occasional extra one is called into special service during the replication actions. With two chains of structural material as sidebars, nature forms rungs of chemical elements, called nucleotides, of equal width. Each rung of the ladder is an element that can attach to the sidebars only according to a simple rule. As formed, the ladder twists about itself according to physical rules, thereby forming the double helix.

The four constituents are all organic bases. They are adenine (A) that bonds only with thymine (T), except that it will also bond with uracil in the replication process, guanine (G), and cytosine (C). I used to tell my students that they—C, G, A, and T—were the most important letters in any language. This is not intended to be a text on genetics, so I will provide only a simple representation of how replication works. You can, however, literally see how genetic change comes about. More information is available from Dawkins or Ridley. A chromosome is shown below.

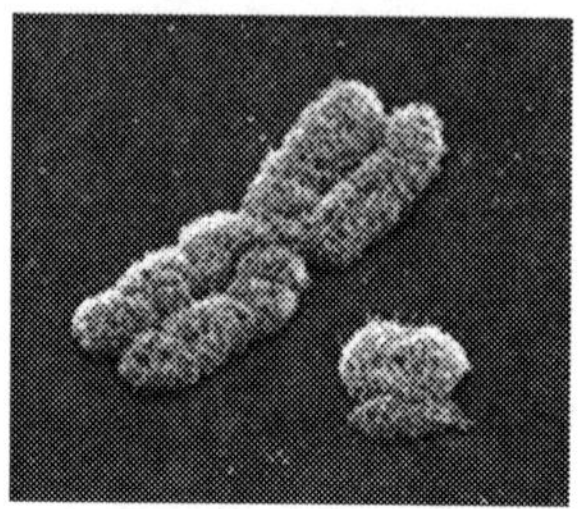

The ladder sides are made of elements that have areas where rungs can be attached. Each rung is made of A, C, G, or T's. As each base can attach only at specific places on the sidebars, a ladder of equal-width rungs is formed. Nature, at specific times and under the control of various enzymes and proteins, causes the ladders to unzip serially along their axes. Then each sidebar, now unattached, scoops up the appropriate base element (A, C, G, or T) from the environment, using other specialized elements, and constructs two new ladders exactly the same as the originals. Each is a copy of the original parts. This division is the first step in replication.

Let me describe the process as follows:[30]
Imagine that we are in the realm of sexual reproduction so that each gene in the male and the female gene or the individual complete ladder is mixed or brought into contact. This can be likened to a word, shown here as one word in upper case representing the female gene, and the other in lower case writing represent-

ing the male gene—"CHANGING" and "changing." Move these so we can better illustrate:

CHANGING-female gene
changing—male gene

The first activity (replication), results in the copying of each gene—the helix unzips and an exact copy is made:

CHANGING
CHANGING

changing
changing

But that is not all. If it were, we would exist like simple amoeba, with infinitely long lives as copies of each other—immortal but fixed forever.[31] There is another change that nature organizes—and this is the part of which Darwin knew nothing. This change is a shuffling of the parts among the elements of the gene (word) so that not only is there replication but there is also the possibility of change and the creation of new genes and new species. This process provides the possibility of creating new types of life through creating new "words." In the mundane world we live in, the shuffling of genes results in children that often differ greatly from their parents. Change is the essential element of evolution and it comes about like this: within the "cell" illustrated here, there are the four parts shown above in lower and upper case. Amazingly, two of these four parts exchange bits with each other and create new words as follows:
CHANging—new word
CHANGING—original word
chanGING—new word
changing—original word

Consequently, if these were people, we would get two new words and retain two old ones:

CHANging—the offspring
CHANGING—original female genes, Mother

chanGING—another offspring
changing—original male genes, Father

We now have two children, CHANGing and chanGING, that differ from their parents in their genetic make-up, each being a part of each parent. In actuality, there may be other shuffling orders as well and the subsequent chance of random effects that may induce changes within each.

This shuffling through sexual selection is the key to evolution, as it not only preserves the basic pattern of the original elements, but it also introduces new ones that will influence the future development of the gene. Genes actually determine the sort of person we are. However, lest you should misunderstand, the brain may override the general directions of the genome in any particular case that does not involve fundamental processes.

One can see that in a population of thousands, some changes in genes might arise through the effects of solar radiation changing some chromosome elements, perhaps a certain arrangement that will produce, say, a taller or stronger person, or one who will be more disease resistant. Together with other random changes, over time, such alterations would lead to some individuals being better survivors (specifically in the days when disease was a frequent killer), while those without the genetic change would sicken and, over time, become a smaller and smaller part of the population. Again, over time the new population would be deemed fitter, because the progeny of the earlier population had been displaced by the better-adapted descendents. We can readily see this process with bacteria because they reproduce at such a high rate. When an antibiotic is introduced into a Petrie dish colony of bacteria, most will die. Some, having a slight variation from the "normal" genetic make-up, can survive. Those survivors will soon reproduce and be resistant to the antibiotic—that is evolution on a Petrie dish! That is also how we are able to recognize disease-resistant organisms.

Adaptation of organisms to specific conditions—here temperature change is noted—is also possible. We in the Eastern U.S. experienced, in the springtime of 2004, the reappearance of the cicadas—the 17-year cicadas. Since Colonial days, people have wondered why this regularity occurred; could cicadas count? It appears that they have learned to count for self-preservation. A study showed clearly that the cicada population would suffer extinction if they appeared all at the same time—that indeed would be a feast for predators. Over the millenniums, the cicadas that appeared only at 13- or 17-year cycles had the best chance of surviving and of passing on their genes to the next generation and thereby preserving the population.

Data and simulations showed that, over a 1,500 year period in which one of 50 summers was cold enough to be fatal to emerging cicadas, those insects with life cycles of from two to seven years, during this period, would have seen only 1% to 8% of them surviving. Life cycles of 17 years for the cicadas would, under the same conditions, see 96% of all cicadas having a chance of surviving. For 13-year cicadas, the survival rate was estimated to be 74%.[32] Consequently, it does appear that cicadas can count. By having nature arrange the fact that large numbers also appeared in the 13th year, the chances of survival were made better for the genes of all cicadas. Having two such populations appear at an interval minimizes the chances of the extirpation of all cicadas, either by predation or by a change in the cycle of killing temperatures.

In addition to reproduction, other things assist the continuation of evolution through genetic variation. These mechanisms involve mutation, which was mentioned above under a change in the DNA sequence in a gene; genetic drift, as when small, random changes in an individual gene eventually affect the population; gene flow, as when population movement occurs so that new genes are available for reproduction, or when, for plants, seeds are blown to new areas. Natural selection and sexual selection introduce additional means of varying the human genome.

There is another evolutionary process that is also at work and that is usually minimized in importance, but it may have great strength in the evolution of culture. This is called "Baldwinian" evolution—where learning, behavior and the environment influence natural selection. The theory accepts that there is a genetic transmission of characteristics, but states that there is also social transmission, and that the overall environment is a source of physical persistence of change. There are feed-back effects among genes, behavior, and the environment.

To quote a recent, well-received book, *The Symbolic Species—Co-evolution of Language and the Brain*, by Terrence W. Deacon—Baldwin proposed that, by temporarily adjusting behavior or psychological responses during its lifespan in response to novel conditions, an animal could produce irreversible changes in the adaptive context of future generations. Although no new genetic change is immediately produced in the process, the change in conditions will alter which among the existing or subsequently modified genetic predispositions will be favored in the future. The chart illustrates the process.[33]

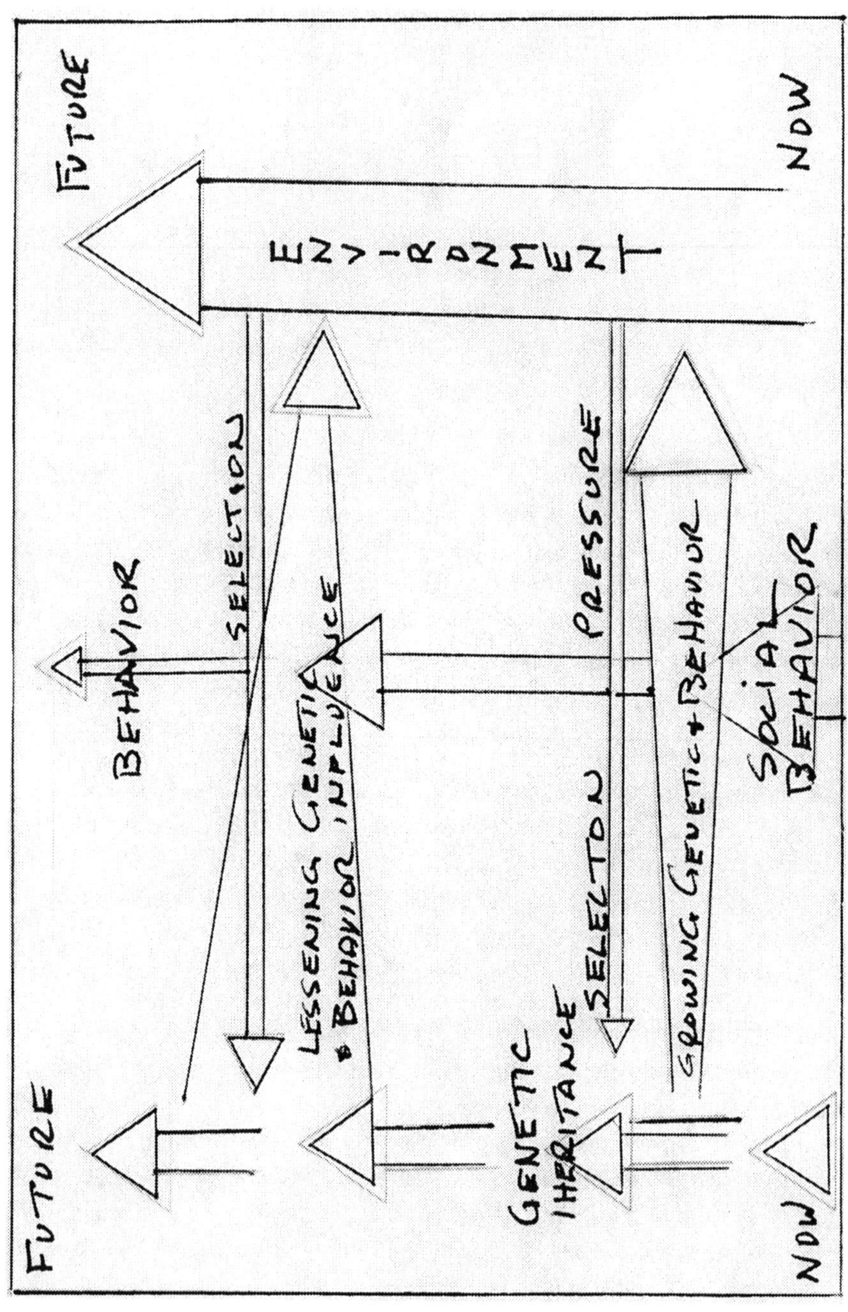
FUTURE
NOW
ENVIRONMENT
SELECTION
PRESSURE
BEHAVIOR
LESSENING GENETIC INFLUENCE
& BEHAVIOR
SELECTION
GROWING GENETIC + BEHAVIOR
SOCIAL BEHAVIOR
GENETIC INHERITANCE
FUTURE
NOW

This diagram, based upon the work of Terrence W. Deacon's "The Symbolic Species: the co-evolution of language and the brain" (Norton, 1997) and Bruce H. weber and David J. Depew, "Evolution and Learning: The Baldwin Effect Reconsidered" (MIT Prerss, 2003). The influences are simultaneous through time.

Genetic influence remains constant but the influence of behavior on evolution first increases then decreases over time as shown by smaller arrows. Behavioral influences on environment, growing at first, decrease over time. Environmental influences on genes remain constant.

Ultimately, natural selection may or may not lead a population to having an optimal set of traits. In any population, there would be a certain combination of possible genes that would lead to an optimum. However, there are also other sets of genes that might lead to a closely adapted part of a population or to a local optimum. The influences of social and environmental factors can, over time, produce a population through these feed-back effects that is on the road to an optimum situation.

But the concept of an adaptive landscape may be of use here. Imagine a landscape with two hills, one high and the other lower, separated by a low valley. If natural selection had created a population, one part on the lower and one, much better adapted, on the higher hill, it would be very difficult (in evolutionary terms) for a transition to be made from lower to higher without having to pass through the valley—in evolutionary terms, going backward. Those that have successfully reached the high hill have already passed through the valley—a constraint that is likened to severe conditions where only a few of a given population (those better adapted) survive.

Such constraints have been put on humanity in the distant past when as few as, perhaps, a few thousand humans of our ancestors survived. These claims can be traced through the disappearance of many genetic markers and the survival of other markers in our population. Some of the missing markers are to be found in other populations that did not migrate out of Africa.

This is about all I will say about evolution—it affects whole populations that are better adapted to their niche of living; those populations less adapted than others disappeared from history. Fittest, in Darwinian terms, means the ability of a population to reproduce itself after adapting to changed circumstances. The survival of the fittest applies to populations, not individuals who have a shorter life than the whole population and within which small adaptive changes cannot readily be seen. The gene is a self-replicating entity driven by chemical and other influences to endlessly continue to replicate, leaving behind a record of its travels through genetic markers that are carried to this day. In fact, by concentrating on the specific genetic make-up of elements carried only within females, the mitochondria or the powerhouse of the cell, scientists have been able to trace a female line originating in Africa some 200,000 years ago, that gave rise to all living humans.[34] Other human lines have succumbed in ancient or more recent times to a variety of causes—disease, starvation, war, abandonment, etc. We are, thus, all distantly related. We are all survivors. Let us now move on to see how evolution may have changed our minds.

Evolutionary Psychology

Darwin's prediction, made in the final pages of *Origin of the Species,* was that "Psychology will be based on a new foundation, that of the necessary acquirement of each mental power and capacity by gradation." William James, only 30 years later, published his *Principles of Psychology,* which helped found experimental psychology and began to look into the reasons for the instincts of humans.

What is evolutionary psychology or EP?[35] How is it relevant to mythology? EP involves a different way of looking at psychology and human nature. As noted previously, EP may be considered a sub-set of evolutionary biology or neo-Darwinism. EP provides evidence of general biological tendencies that interact with an individual's environment. We evolved physically to solve a number of common problems that arose in our evolutionary environment; equally, we have developed psychological skills to operate in the environment of our evolutionary ancestors. There has been a lot of time to do this since proto-humans had basic instincts that were passed on through the two million years since *Homo habilis* began to chip flints and until there appeared the fully-formed and sentient human we now call *Homo sapiens.* A glance at the tables below will make this clear.

Dates and Geographic Distribution of Major Hominoid and Hominid Fossil Groups

Fossil Group	*Dates (millions years ago)*	*Area*
Hominoids		
Dryopiths	30–10	East Africa & Europe
Ramapiths	19–7	Africa, Asia & Europe
Hominids		
Australopithecines		Africa
A. afarensis	3.8–3.0	East Africa
Robusts		
A. robustus	3–2?	South Africa
A. boisei	2.5?–1.2	East Africa
Graciles		
A. africanus	3–2?	S. (&E?) Africa
Homo		
H. Habilis	2.0–1.6	East Africa
H. Erectus	1.6–0.3	Africa, Asia & Europe
H. Sapiens		
Earliest H.S. (including)	0.3–.13 (300,000–130,000)	Africa, Asia & Europe
Archaic H.S.	0.13–0.035 (130,000–35,000)	Africa, Asia & Europe
Homo Sapiens Neanderthalensis	0.075–0.035 (75,000–35,000)	Europe & Middle East
Homo Sapiens Sapiens	0.035?–present (35,000–present	Worldwide

During the past two million years, humans developed ways to deal with their environment. From creating simple tools, and improving them, to creating art and rituals that indicate the very beginnings of religious inclination, they prospered. They did this because various traits, which were honed through time, assisted their continued existence.

One must realize that there are no "selfish genes." It makes as much sense to say that atoms or electrons have purpose as it does to state that genes are selfish. A set of genes creates proteins that, at the urgings of certain chemicals, create an organism with no consciousness, which is an attribute of a large brain and exists only in a vestigial form among animals. The groups of genes of which we are comprised bear only the urge to reproduce. They do that in various ways—from the divisions of simple organisms to the copulations of animals—the modes of reproduction are myriad. Consider the butterfly!

Therefore, it is only the collection of genes that has purpose. At the simplest level, reproduction is the stamp of nature upon genes. The environment within which the genes operate determines their fate. Were Darwin to write in modern English, he might have said, "Those traits that confer a survival advantage over those without that trait will survive to breed more often and that trait will become more common in that population of animals."

For humans, the relevant environment was mainly that of other humans—a social environment, not a physical one. Our brains, minds, and bodies took on their current configuration (or the totality of all factors impinging upon humans), during the Pleistocene era of the world. This took place approximately a million years ago, during what is called The Environment of Evolutionary Adaptedness (EEA). During this period, our human ancestors lived in small bands of hunter-gatherers within stable social groups, with which they had repeated interactions, over relatively long life spans. The main concerns were with interactions with other humans and the dangers they faced. Humans have essentially the same biological nature now as they did then.

Cultural change, that is equivalent to environmental change, has, however, been very rapid over the past 80,000 years. Consequently, a mind used to dealing with ancient problems may be stressed by having to deal with the unfamiliar problems of developing and changing cultures. A mismatch has thus developed between handling the essential problems and drives of ancient minds and solving the newer, developing problems of changing cultures.

For modern political philosopher, F. A. Hayek (1899–1992), the purpose of culture and institutions is to control our self-destructive tendencies, to impose our small-group sentiments on modern society. Thomas Hobbes (1588–1679) claimed, in his book, *Leviathan,* that without a powerful central authority, the state of nature would be a war of "all against all." EP suggests that four mechanisms have arisen to show that cooperation among humans may be the evolutionary selected course.[36]

These are: (1) kin selection, wherein close kin are favored in order to permit closely genetically related persons to survive; (2) cooperation for mutual advantage, which is a form of altruistic behavior where cooperation, in say hunting groups, will result in a greater total benefit than otherwise; (3) reciprocal altruism, a longer-term variant of self-interest where the mutual gains from reciprocal altruism are produced over time. (I give you a benefit in the expectation that you will reciprocate in the future.) It appears that there may be two other general types of altruism—genetic altruism and behavioral altruism.

Behavioral altruism is a pattern of behavior in which a biological entity enhances the wellbeing of another entity at its own expense. This includes kin altruism, noted previously, in which a parent's wellbeing is sacrificed or reduced on behalf of its offspring; reciprocal altruism in which a sacrifice is made by one party so as to be repaid at some time in the future by the other party, indirect reciprocity in which one individual's sacrifice on behalf of another is repaid by a third party, and strong reciprocity in which humans sacrifice on behalf of unrelated third parties with no expectation of future pay-back. These last few examples may be extended to having altruistic expectations on people of similar ethnicity[37] or acquaintance outside of the kin-group. Genetic altruism occurs when the expression, or coming into action, of a gene reduces the frequency of the gene in the population—by this definition, genetic altruism cannot exist in the long run. A little thought will give a clear understanding of how the ideas of EP are related to common occurrences in families, tribes, groups, and nations.

A fourth element—group selection—is the most controversial of the above elements. It holds out the possibility of cooperation on a society-wide basis. Group selection comes in two types: biological and cultural or environmental. On the one hand, under certain conditions it may be adaptive on the individual level to develop altruistic traits toward others. Altruism builds trust and reciprocity and reduces the transaction costs of a larger society; it spurs trade, specialization, and growing wealth.

Such populations tend to prosper at the expense of less hearty populations and gradually displace non-altruistic populations among the groups that comprised early man. Cultural group selection has similar arguments, except instead of propagating genetic traits, the selection propagates through "*memes.*" *Memes* are, in this context, the rules, customs, institutions, and norms of the group. Groups that adopt "better" cultural practices will grow healthier, wealthier, and more populous—they will tend to displace less efficient cultures through conquest, migration, adoption or inclusion. The *memes* thus replicate in society as cultural practices accepted by many and finally, by all. In many senses, religion is propagated through *memes*, as is myth, which we have identified as a constituent of religiosity.

Hayek suggests that, for group selection to be viable, there must be some benefit to the group from the trait or practice considered; there must be some mechanism for the inter-group competition to take place; and that there must be some mechanism to police "free riding" in order to prevent some from claiming a share of the social surplus without contributing to it. Cultural systems provide these functions. They appear to work in the manner described earlier regarding Baldwinian evolution.

These elements suggest that religiosity involves, on a personal and on a group level, most of the above elements that define EP. Mysticism, in the days of the hunter-gatherer, involved dealing with the mysterious and with fear. Because the human brain was adapted to receive inputs that satisfied the underlying receptivity to religiosity, a sense of wonder and of the inexplicable and uncertain was created. A human brain that was able to make inferential suppositions could then readily seek or create explanations for the mysteries of the world.

What could not be explained obviously was, as has been shown earlier, relegated to the sphere of religion. Many believed that it was in the nature of humanity to have religion—it was human nature.

Human Nature

The long-standing and current view of human nature has become powerful and pervasive, reaching into all aspects of contemporary society and distorting a proper understanding of our own humanity. It is necessary to understand how the structure of thought related to human nature is changing so we can make an assessment of the view that mythology and human nature are closely related. The new 21st Century paradigm concerning human nature will enable us to appreciate how mythology can be regarded as arising from the most fundamental and genetic constituents of humanity.

Many recent views about human nature are founded, at least in the Jewish, Christian and Muslim worlds (the religions of the book) in religion and are evident in Hinduism (the myths) and in Buddhism, but not in Taoism or Confucianism.[38] The view that man and animals are basically different; that women are subordinate to men; that the mind exists after death; that the mind has specific areas devoted to love, morals, reason, good and evil; that sinfulness derives from ancient acts; that there is inherent sinfulness; and that the Biblical and the Koranic narratives are literally true—all derive from religion. But there is more—humans throughout the ages and in all stages of civilization have developed views about the relationship between the individual and the cosmos. It can be seen that there is a convergence between Eastern and Western views about the cosmos, upon a generally common set of ideas that include modern ideas about reality. An Appendix deals with this matter.

Just prior to the 1600s, human nature in the Christian and Muslim worlds was derived solely from scripture. When humans fell from grace, or were sinful, they always had the scripture, as interpreted by priests or respected scholars, to fall back on for redemption in this life. Certain life experiences or actions also conferred a heavenly afterlife or determined everlasting hell—always defined as a variety of nasty situations. The importance of this must not be underestimated either in relationship to restraining the baser elements of humans or as providing a source of comfort in those most uncertain and unhealthy times. Of course, the religious precepts were often backed by swift and terrible worldly sanctions for miscreants—but not often in rewards in this life.

Before the beginning of the 17th Century, humans in the Christian West were thought to be mired in sin and they behaved, through religious practices and confession, according to the views of various Christian Churches. It was the general attitude among most Christians, Roman, Orthodox, and others, that the ethics and the rules of the Church should be abided. Changes were coming though; and it is useful at this point, to step back and consider how our current and usual view of human nature arose.

Until recently, most studies in the West related to the humanities and the natural sciences were dependent upon approaches that were developed during the period called The Enlightenment. It is a term that refers to the questions and activities by certain people by which ideas about God, reason, nature, and science, were synthesized into a new paradigm during the 100 years between the end of the English Revolution of 1688 and the French Revolution of 1789.

As a result of The Enlightenment, the goals of rational man were considered to be knowledge, freedom, and happiness. This synthesis triggered many new developments in the arts, the sciences, philosophy, and politics, which continued almost to the end of World War II. Men threw off the restrictions that had been imposed by churches and by the guiding notions of society. God, however, continued to have an honored place in all areas, including the religious household and the childhood of Charles Darwin.

This period of Western history grew out of the questioning of the autocratic views of the Catholic Church.[39] These concerned the centrality of the Earth in the heavens and the role of God. Copernicus' view that the heavens were like a machine, and the heretical view of Galileo, in 1610, that the world was not the center of the heavens. This questioning opened the door for the questioning in all manner of human activity previously closed by the Church. Over successive years, the questioning of the biblical views of man and nature continued in many fields in the Western world. There were basically two areas, philosophy and science, where this questioning produced profound results.

In philosophy and in the realm of politics, one can recognize several groups or schools—exponents of "just order," such as Milton and Hobbes, (1651) who said that, "Everyman is presumed to seek that which is good for himself naturally, and what is just only for Peaces sake and accidentally;" rationalists like Descartes, Vico, and Leibniz; "empiricists" such as Newton, Boyle, and Locke; and the "revolutionaries," such as Paine, Franklin, Burke, Hamilton and Jefferson, who so greatly influence our lives today.

For our purposes here, none is more influential in the field of human relations than John Locke (1632). He believed that there were no innate qualities in humans and that all were born as "Blank Slates," or *tabula rasa,* upon which experience wrote the character of an individual. His ideas are to be found in his book, *On Human Understanding.* The idea that society, the Bible, the family, and the state, could be the major influences upon a person, created an entire view of the proper relations between the individual and the outside world—the source of the writing on the Blank Slate! This idea influenced politics, personal relations and the law from that time forward, almost until the present.

The empiricists believed that the senses and experiments were the path to knowledge. Isaac Newton, the most important member of this group, offered the view that nature could be discovered through mathematics and that there was no need for God as an explanation of nature. These views, disseminated by a growing press, greatly influenced Western thought and political developments. Many others also questioned the established orders, changed political structures, and opened literature to much wider and questioning views.

Similar changes were at work in science. Because of the invention of the microscope, scientists like Robert Hooke were able to see cells and to discover a world within a drop of puddle-water. This curiosity was grasped by many and it spurred the science of biology and chemistry. Medicine, too, benefited from the new questioning attitude with William Harvey, an early discoverer of the circulation of the blood, and Edward Jenner, who rediscovered the Arab's method of inoculation for smallpox. Much earlier information, lost during the Dark Ages, was recovered and widely disseminated through the printing press.

There were immense changes brought about through a more questioning attitude on the part of many people. The questioning expanded into all spheres of life and eventually resulted, after discoveries and inventions in metallurgy and organization, in what we now call the Industrial Revolution that swept through Britain, Europe, and America to the beginning of the Twentieth Century.

The concept of the human personality as a blank slate, capable of being molded by social, cultural, legal, and economic forces, has ruled much of the way humans regard each other. This view was originally proposed by John Locke in 1690 and embellished by many others until it became embedded in the social sciences. It has dominated many aspects of modern life in social legislation, for example, in laws affecting children, the common law, and politics, where Communism famously based itself upon the molding, and improvement of society.

Other ideas about humans were contained in the concept of the Noble Savage, propounded by Jean-Jacques Rousseau in *The Social Contract* (1762). This idea was that humans were basically peaceful and that, if left alone, would prosper. Contesting this sentiment, were the views of Thomas Hobbes, whose book, *Leviathan,* published in 1651, stated that man, left alone, would experience a life that was, "... solitary, poor, nasty, brutish, and short." Man, therefore should be controlled by a superior force—the law, the state, or some great power.

Finally, the notion that God was supreme was supposedly proven by the mathematician and philosopher Rene Descartes (1596–1650). He, rejecting all ideas based on assumptions or emotional beliefs and accepting only what could be proven, considered that the mind could not operate on mechanical principles. He then posited that the mind and body were controlled by the Ghost in the Machine—God. Despite set backs, the questioning of the established order continued in philosophy and science, particularly in the Muslim areas where advances in mathematics and the sciences, although not questioning the words of the Koran, were eventually transferred to the West, providing a basis for further advances in science and mathematics. It was in philosophy that the greatest impact on the world of law and social doctrine was made, as ancient Greek texts were translated to Latin from Arabic and made available to Western scholars.

Nonetheless, for most of the recent past, the concept of human nature as a blank slate existed, and still exists. People were capable of being molded by social, cultural, legal, and economic forces. The concept has dominated the West and has been responsible for many aspects of social life, legislation, laws, and politics.

Many recent expositors of this view of human nature became influential in the universities and came to dominate thought in sociology and in other humanities. One such leader in the social sciences was Franz Boas (1858–1942), who said, "I claim that we must assume that all complex activities are socially determined, not hereditary." Among his influential and prominent students were Margaret Mead and Ruth Benedict, who came to dominate American social science. They believed in social determinism and that culture was super-organic, so that heredity could not be allowed to have any part in history.

Another doyen of social science in the United States, Emil Durkheim (1858–1917), wrote, "Every time a social phenomenon is directly explained by a psychological phenomenon, we may be sure that the explanation is false." All of social science denied that the mind was important and stated that ideas, thoughts, and plans arose from language. All shared a dislike of Darwin and evolution, while accepting that the sorts of inherited changes in flowers and plants described by Gregor Mendel (1882–1886) were passed from generation to generation. The slate was blank, but the mind was malleable and the tiny individual mind was not to be considered except as part of a vast socio-cultural system. One recent and currently held view of human nature, called behaviorism, rejected the study of mental processes as unscientific and extended its application to the Blank Slate Model.

Evolution and the Darwinian modifications provided by the science of the 20th Century would not go away. It became clear during these years that there was much left to learn about humanity. Chromosomes had been seen through much more powerful microscopes; new information about cells and the nucleus became available. All that was lacking to begin to better understand human nature was the information provided in 1953 by James Watson and Francis Crick—a description of the basis of the human genome as a Double Helix.[40] Biblical scholars will recall the incredible analogy to *Jacob's* ladder in Genesis 28.12.

The application of modern Darwinian ideas about evolution to the study of human society began, one might say, with the 1975 publication of *Sociobiology: The New Synthesis*, by E. O. Wilson. He is an eminent scientist who made his reputation through a study of insects and their habitats. His book advanced the idea that all human activity is genetically based and should be called sociobiology, as there were obvious and strong evolutionary elements in biological operations. This idea was greeted with a fire-storm of opposition and much of it was directed, not at the book, but at Wilson personally. He was seen as intruding on established fields of scholarly work and he was physically attacked. Subsequently, and perhaps as a reaction to the criticism, sociobiology came to be called evolutionary biology, of which evolutionary psychology, or EP, is a sub-set. Wilson went on to write another book, called *On Human Nature,* which opposed the idea of the blank slate but echoed the title of John Locke's publication of 1690.[41]

While most individuals were persuaded readily by the evidence that evolutionary biology provides a sensible explanation of the biological nature of humans—two arms and two legs, warm blooded, upright, with vision and hearing, and symmetrical—it was much more difficult for scholars to be reconciled to the idea that evolution has psychological consequences. Nonetheless, the evidence against the old ideas of human nature was impressive.

After Wilson's book, there was soon a rapidly growing number of studies exploring the implications of the new findings—the sequencing of the entire human genome and the growing experimental use of brain imaging scans—and their implications. Popular writers from within the field of genomics and other sciences contributed to a wider understanding and spread of information about the growing interrelationship of all sciences. Among these writers, was the biologist, Richard Dawkins (*The Selfish Gene*), who claimed that the gene was the principal unit of natural selection in evolution and that all living bodies had only the function of replicating the genes. I[42] Daniel Dennett, a leading figure in the philosophy of the mind and of science and important in fields related to evolutionary biology and cognitive science, contributed *Darwin's Dangerous Idea* and *Con-*

sciousness Explained. Another worthwhile writer is Matt Ridley who wrote the popular books *Genome: The Autobiography of a Species in 23 Chapters* and *Nature Via Nurture: Genes, Experience, and What Makes Us Human.*

Such writings really put the cat among the pigeons in the various associated fields. Dawkins' view of evolution may be called "ultra-Darwinist," since it seems rather digital or technologically focused (in fact he included a computer program in one of his books). His book features "robots" and "vehicles" and DNA, not flesh and blood people and animals. The thrust of his argument was that humans are vehicles for propagating their genes. A biting review of *The Selfish Gene* by Richard Lewontin, of Harvard and published in *Nature,* spoke of "Dawkins' discovery of vulgar Darwinism." It was blindly and naively optimistic wrote Lewontin, "... to think that all describable behavior must be the direct product of natural selection." In the ensuing debate, paragons of learning in the biological and physical sciences were lined up, often on opposite sides of the Atlantic.[43]

Consequently, it is appropriate to look at what the neurological scientist Steven Pinker (of the Brain and Cognitive Science group at MIT) has to say about the change toward human nature in his book, *The Blank Slate.*[44] He writes smoothly, humorously and well and he destroys the idea of the blank slate in three chapters. Pinker says that a new conception of human nature, which is connected to biology, can also be connected to the humanities and the social sciences. This is where we will find our interests.

Steven Pinker says that the unification of human sciences in the new understanding of matter and energy is, "the greatest achievement of the 20th Century." This unification has given rise to cognitive science, cognitive neuroscience, behavioral genetics, evolutionary biology and evolutionary psychology. Interest in these fields has been spurred by the Internet. For example, there are currently 6,870,000 documents on evolutionary psychology online: 90,200 Google Scholar book documents: and hundreds of new journals and papers in many languages, all devoted to the new areas of study in the biological sciences.

Pinker says that the way to consider the new blending of the sciences is to look at the following ways that science, genetics and neural studies are now used to illuminate human nature:

(A) Biology and Culture may be related via cognitive science

There are five ideas from the cognitive revolution that undermine the concept of the blank slate and the existence of God. These are:

1. The mind cannot be a blank slate because, if it were, it could do nothing. Something in the mind is innate and that thing is a learning mechanism.

2. The mental and physical world can be related by concepts of information that reside in patterns within the brain. Thinking and planning transform those patterns and create feedback loops. The mind is connected to sense organs by activities that change physical energy into data structures and by motor programs that control muscles. If transformations of information mirror a series of deductions that obey laws of probability, logic, and cause and effect, they will generate correct predictions about the world. If the prediction is incorrect, the entity will not succeed or it will die. So, intelligence is the pursuit of a goal.

3. An infinite range of behavior can be gotten through finite combinatorial processes. As the brain has some billion neurons, there are infinite ways that neural combinations can be used to learn and to solve problems. This is information use.[45]

4. Universal mental mechanisms underlie variations across cultures. Language has a structure that obeys certain laws. For example, the "head first" or "head last" structure of sentences seems to affect about 95% of languages. The sentence, "I heard rumors that you are leaving town," in English-based languages becomes, in Japanese "I, that you are leaving town, rumors heard."

5. The mind is a complex system of interacting parts—universal generative computational modules—and humans have flexibility because they are programmed to use combinatorial approaches to produce an unlimited set and range of thoughts and behaviors.

(B) Neuroscience also relates mind and matter

Thoughts, feelings, aches, dreams, wishes, and regrets are all psychological activities in the brain. Cognitive neuroscientists have shown not only that there is no Ghost in the Machine—no God—but also that there is no review of the facts of thoughts or of actions of an order to carry out actions. When the joining between the two hemispheres of the brain, the *corpus callosum,* is cut, each half operates as a sort of independent brain. For example, after such an operation a specific side of the brain can be isolated by putting a patch over one eye so that the individual's isolated brain-part cannot "see" the result of an action. When given a written order to, "Walk over to the cooler and take a drink," the individual carries out the order. Then, when the other side of the brain is free to see the result and is asked, "Why did you get the water?" it makes up a reason for the thirst and the result of the action. Not only is the mind a "spin doctor," our minds do not control how we act, but they make up stories or a rationale for our actions. Such experiments, often conducted by having a supposed criminal run through a lecture hall and then asking the witnesses to describe the miscreant, are given to law students. The results are uniformly failures, but they may have implications for the law.[46]

(C) Biology and mental activity are related via behavioral genetics—how genes affect behavior. Slight differences in an individual's DNA composition can lead to differences in activities. An example can be seen in the differences that genes have on language. The absence of certain parts of genes can lead, for example, to the inability to speak. While most effects of genetic changes between generations are benign, many can be deleterious. New findings have also led to the identification of disease causes. For example, if a tiny part of chromosome 22 is missing (called *22Ql1.2 deletion syndrome)* symptoms such as heart defects, cleft palate, cognitive impairment and abnormal immune response can occur. Genes also can randomly move among chromosomes. This was discovered in maize (corn) by Barbara McClintock in 1983. It earned her the Nobel Prize. Genes can also be affected by environment. In the case of corn, the height of corn grown in different soils can affect future generations. All five types of personalities (introvert-extrovert, neurotic-stable, curious-uncurious, agreeable-antagonistic, and conscientious-undirected) are inheritable, with 50% of a population's personality types related to gene differences. Studies of identical and fraternal twins also show striking similarities and a few differences leading to the question, "How much free will is there?"

Behavioral genetics has also debunked the entire idea of "The Noble Savage"-the idea that mankind left in its own primitive state would develop and lead a peaceful and prosperous life. Not only is a Noble Savage unlikely to appear because of Darwinian evolution, but data from primitive societies also shows that in South America and New Guinea from 20% to 40% of males were regularly killed in warfare. In the 20th Century, including the U.S. and Europe during the period of the two World Wars, it appears that around 5% of all their adult males were killed.[47] Pre-state societies were even bloodier than modern. Thomas Hobbes, in

1651, predicted that humanity, left alone, would lead a life that was "nasty, brutish, and short." He was correct.

(D) Biology and culture are related via evolutionary psychology—the study of phylogenic (species) history and the adaptive functions of the mind. Real time actions and activities may be tied to the ultimate reasons for certain actions—thus the need for nutrition and reproduction gives rise to a drive to overcome hunger and a drive for lust. The mind is crammed with cravings, many of which are related to the propagation of the species, shaped by natural selection and a generic desire for personal wellbeing.

So it seems clear that the new human sciences are both dependent upon evolutionary studies and draw upon modern science.

The finding and identification of Human Universals[48]—over 400 to date—within all societies, indicate that there are commonalities among all people derived from their common genetic make-up and history. The identification of human universals leads to the clear possibility that the concept of the "collective unconscious" and "archetypes," first assumed by Carl Jung in a psychological framework, has merit. The idea that natural selection has endowed humanity with a universal complex mind gets more support from child psychologists, archaeologists, and brain researchers, who see similarities in human actions in their fields.

As will be suggested later, all human minds seem to develop a relatively standard set of reasoning and regulatory circuits, functionally specialized and thought to be specific to various domains of the brain. These 'domains' may, however, only be collection points—way stations—in a network of neurons. Through their immense combinatorial powers, these circuits organize and interpret the way we react to our experiences. In addition to their general 'housekeeping' tasks—blood pressure control, balance, endocrine regulation, etc, they inject certain recurrent concepts and motivations into our mental life and provide frames of meaning that allow us to understand the actions and intentions of others. There are innate areas, too. For example, the innate ability to construct languages—most of which have a common underlying structure—is a mechanism for learning language. This learning mechanism also provides humans with the ability to discern the intentions of other people, as can be seen with even very young children who will not repeatedly copy the mistakes of others in play. Our minds are, then, equipped with the means to infer and read the intentions of others. Our minds, too, are able to deal with recursive sentences and ideas—the ability to consider imaginary events. This is an evolutionary inheritance and was essential, in various ways, to the continuation of the species.

It is reasonable to suggest that evolutionary psychology can be explained through responses to such universals. If one is responsive to mysticism, music, art, and other symbolic indications, then one is ready to react appropriately to presented symbols and to act accordingly. This can lead to the concepts of the collective unconscious and of elementary ideas, introduced into the literature of sociology and psychology by Adolf Bastian in 1860. His concept of *elemental ideas* was the trigger that caused psychologist Carl Jung, then a student of Sigmund Freud, to explore these themes and further elaborate upon them.

Working well before modern times and the new understanding of EP, Jung, using concepts borrowed from Bastian, developed the view, somewhat similar to that of Brown's, that there are certain human universals, called "archetypes" or symbols. These elicit strong reactions or associations within individuals through what Jung labeled the "collective unconscious," but that we might call brain circuitry. In Jung's judgment, this resource was a "psychic inheritance," a reservoir of human experience as a species, although he could not explain how this inheritance came about. Jung also proposed and developed the concepts of the extroverted and introverted personality. His work has been influential in psychiatry and in the study of religion, literature, and related fields including mythology. Between 1907 and 1912, Jung was a collaborator with Sigmund Freud, but they disagreed when Jung published *The Psychology of the Unconscious,* which deprecated Freud's heavy emphasis on sexuality.

The archetype, claimed Jung, acts on the things we see and do only as an organizing principle. Symbols related to certain elementary occurrences seemed to be, retained among all humans. These became triggers to recall events and meanings for an individual. He called these events "Innate Releasing Mechanisms *(IRM),*" and gave examples in the animal and human kingdoms. Joseph Campbell gives, as an example of this theory of IRMs, the alarm that newly hatched chicks have to the image of a hawk above but not to that of other bird forms.[49] As another example of this theory, we can observe the power of the swastika to cause a reaction—a common symbol that has been used by humans for at least 5,500 years, well before the rise of Adolph Hitler. It was used and seen in earlier times in the Americas as well as in the Near East and Europe.[50] It is found in pre-Columbian

America, among the Hindu; in central Asia; and throughout ancient Europe. I shall use this concept of a 'trigger' again when discussing the brain.

The route, I believe, to understanding the origin, development and importance of mythology lies through a grasp of the new field of evolutionary biology and evolutionary psychology. While evolutionary biology attempts to show how the biological/physical aspects of living things, including humans, evolved (it is a prime discipline, of course, depends upon an understanding of current evolutionary theories in the field of the paleo-anthropologist and the archaeologist), evolutionary psychology attempts to describe the underlying mental developments of humans that make the species unique.

To this point, this writing has set out a number of suppositions: that myths are, through *memes* and stories, part of learning passed on for many years; that magic and the mystical/supernatural were the breeding grounds for the appearance of various sorts of formal religions; and that there are grounds for suggesting that the recall of events results from the existence of a symbolic machinery within the brains of humans.

3

HUMANITY'S TRAVELS—CONSTRAINTS AND OPPORTUNITIES

Primitive, slouching creatures, now named Homo Erectus, originated in Africa some 4.0 million years ago[51/52] and gradually spread out over the contiguous land mass of Africa. About 2.0 million years ago these creatures, in search of food, were enticed and constrained (and sometimes eliminated through starvation) by changes in climate as they moved about, eventually entering and accessing all of what came to be known as the Asian and European land mass. Throughout these millions of years, many types of animals also migrated from continent to continent, utilizing various land bridges that were exposed from time to time by the growing glaciers.

Analysis of 11 human genetic evolutionary trees suggests the following human movements—Homo Erectus is found outside of Africa about 1,700,000 BCE. This exodus was followed by two more such movements, the first of these was about 600,000 BCE and involved the Neanderthals; the second was of Homo Sapiens Sapiens—our ancestors. Despite the repeated and frequent migrations of these early humans, it has been determined that the common ancestor of all living humans lived in Africa about 170,000 BCE.

The climate in those early years fluctuated between cold, dry, warm, and damp. Glaciers were formed that variously affected and stressed humanoid and mammal populations alike. Now known as the Nebraskan/Gunz, Riss and Wurm glaciations, these climatic changes directly influenced all forms of life, including the humans who left Africa. The cold that produced glaciers proceeded inexorably and caused the sea levels to slowly fall as much as 100–150 meters (about 300 feet), and to rise again as the ice melted. Various glaciations and the areas affected are shown, along with their regional names in the table below:

Time (1000 Years)	*Conditions*	*North America*	*Alps*	*Northern Europe*	*Poland-Russia*
0–18	*Interglacial*				
18–67	Glacial	Wisconsin	Wurm	Vistula	Varsovian
67–128	*Interglacial*	*Sangamon*	*Uznach*	*Eem*	*Masovian*
128–180	Glacial	Illinoisan	Riss	Warthe/Saale	Cracovian
180–230	*Interglacial*	*Yarmouth*	*Hoetting*	*Holstein*	*Sandomirian*
230–300	Glacial	Kansan	Mindel	Elster	Jaroslavian
300–330	*Interglacial*	*Aftonian*		*Cromer*	*Likhvin*
330–470	Glacial	"Nebraskan"	Gunz		Menapian
470–540	*Interglacial*			*Waalian*	
540–550	Glacial		Donau II	Weybourne	

This glacial expansion and retreat exposed and covered various land bridges, such as the one joining Scandinavia and the United Kingdom to the French and German coasts in the area known now as the North Sea, the one joining Asia to North America at the Bering Straits, and the one joining together the south-east Asian islands. Also exposed were coastal plains that we now see as oceans or seas with some islands exposed. One of these coastal areas, important to our story, is off the Alaskan Pacific coast. Another may have played a part in the peopling of the western parts of South America.

These changes in sea level during the past 120,000 years could have accounted for the prehistoric peopling of most of the Old World, from Africa, to Europe and mainland Asia. Moving or swimming along the beach, following available crustacean foods, would have been sufficient to carry mankind from the Horn of Africa to Australia and to the islands and mainland of Greece, from the Levant to the Korean Peninsula, and from Singapore to Siberia. When sea levels were low it would have been possible to walk dry-shod from Tripoli and Tunisia to Malta and Sicily; from South Korea to South Japan; from the Sakhalin Peninsula to Hokkaido, North Japan; from Malaysia to Sumatra, Java, and Bali; from Siberia to Alaska over the 500km-wide land connection; and along the shores of North and South America. At some stages and in some places, humans learned to cross the water, even without a land bridge. Java, Bali, and New Guinea were periodically connected to the Asian mainland, so that animals, whose remains have been found, and humans could easily cross to them.

However, the Indonesian island of Flores, isolated by a deep ocean trench, could be reached only by sea crossings, even when the sea level was lowest. Nonetheless, stone tools and fossilized bones on Flores show that humanoids and archaic elephants (Stegodon) must have crossed this deep 19-km-wide, oceanic channel 900,000 to 800,000 years ago. There is no evidence that early people knew how to make boats at that point in history. Either they floated across using tree trunks and logs as rafts, or they swam. The recent (2005) finding of miniature human remains on this island has been explained tentatively by their isolation, ample food, and the lack of predators—all missing evolutionary pressures or selection elements that reduced the need for these humans to acquire larger brains and stature that, in other circumstances, would lead through natural selection to larger physiques. There will be more to this story later.

Another deep oceanic channel—the Strait of Gibraltar—lies between Morocco (in North Africa), Gibraltar and Spain. The strait today is about 13 km at its narrowest point, but when the sea levels of the Atlantic and Mediterranean were lower, the distance across was smaller and a few islands (presently under water) would have appeared. Travel by this route can account for the early appearance of a type of Homo Neanderthal in Spain and Southern France. Fossils from Spain have some traits that seem to be leading in the direction of the Neanderthals.

During most of this time humanoids moved about, all as hunter-gatherers, leaving few traces of their simple activities. The bones and skulls of the Homo Erectus types have been found from Java through China and westward as well as in Europe. This movement of Homo Erectus humanoid types from Africa was indicative of an early exodus. But one can imagine that they and the animals moved about, partly governed in habitation by the fluctuating climate, which, in turn, drove the availability of flora and fauna.

Another derivative from Homo Erectus, called Homo Hidelbergerensis and its relative Homo Neanderthal, appeared some 600,000 BCE in Northern Africa and spread into western Asia and Europe some 200,000 BCE and remained until about 30,000 BCE. After that, for unknown reasons, they disappeared completely—after a decidedly long run. It is speculation that at the time of their exodus from Africa and subsequent outward movements, Neanderthals were blocked from spreading into most of Asia by the lakes formed by the retreat of glaciers. In the meantime, as will be noted below, other Homo Erectus moved throughout Asia and into China some 200,000 BCE. Finally, modern humans, Homo Sapiens, evolved and spread throughout the world, over the millennia beginning about 150,000 BCE.

Under the pressure of changing climate, natural selection drove an increase in intelligence that is reflected in changing cranial capacity. It appears that many of the Homo Erectus and some of the next wave of immigrants from Africa to Asia, Homo Sapiens, were unable to adjust to the new conditions and their populations either vanished or became significantly smaller. The other type of human is called Homo Sapiens Sapiens and it had a bigger brain than its predecessor did. From now on, I will call them Homo Sapiens. They, under the stress of climate change, preserved, through natural selection, the larger brains and that meant greater intelligence and the ability to cope.

The brain capacity of Homo Sapiens is Homo Erectus at about 4½ times the necessary size and other precursors (H. habilis and earlier) with decreasing brain size.[53] After coping with the stresses that drove, through natural selection, increases in brain size to its present capacity, brain size in Homo Sapiens seems to have stabilized around a peaked "normal" distribution.

The movement of humans has been studied recently through chromosomal DNA analysis. Such analysis concentrates on what are called haplotypes, particularly those on the Y-chromosome that escape recombination.[54] These haplotypes are sections of DNA that are hardy and are passed on generation by generation through reproduction. All modern existing Y-chromosomes trace their ancestry to Africa. When Homo Erectus left Africa, it completely replaced various archaic human Y-chromosome lineages in other parts of the world. Using this general method of chromosome study, analysts have traced the ebb and flow of migrations.

There were, in fact, three major movements out-of-Africa (OOA), the first of Homo Erectus about 1.7 million BCE, followed by another about 84K–42K BCE, and a final OOA about 15K–0.8K BCE. Amazingly, there was a reflux of the Homo Sapiens population back into Africa sometime after 10,000 BCE. This move has recently been confirmed through a study of the Berbers of North Africa who have the same genetic signature of an earlier pastoral group from the Middle

East. They also share an origin with the Europeans and Asians, but not with sub-Saharan Africans. Another flow of population from south to north in Europe at about the same time has also been traced and is associated with the fading of the glaciations.

Present day genetic studies of human population movements are currently done through the determination of haplotypes—sections of DNA that are stable through a span of many millenniums. The Y haplotype line that moved OOA, consists of C, D, E, and F haplotype groups. The last, F, includes *nearly* all the other haplogroups—G through R.

The C haplotypes are not found in Africa, implying that these elements evolved prior to the arrival of Homo Erectus in South-East Asia, since C is not found there either. But C is found in the Homo Sapiens in East Asia, Siberia, parts of North America, and in parts of India. This is consistent with, and has been traced to, a movement of humans along the coastlines of Arabia, India, south-east Asia and to Australia; this last reached about 60K BCE. This movement is characterized by the M130 line (part of C) and initially consisted of a very few humans moving along the coasts and living well off foods found on or near the shores.

Here, I must simplify tremendously. These lineages are further divided into many sub-groups. I cannot take the space to describe them in any detail; nevertheless it is interesting to note that the 2,500 year old ice-man, given the name of Otzi, found a few years ago in the Italian Alps, derives from haplogroup K, part of the U-group, which existed at some reasonable level of civilization at that time. Suffice it to say that the general tenor of the most recent findings is given in what follows: The group of C's found in mid-Asia diverged, some going north toward Siberia. From there some moved westward into the north European areas of Finland and north Sweden. Another group leaving Africa moved up and west into Europe through Greece and then westward along the Mediterranean coast.[55] Another of the mid-Asia group diverged northwards into Siberia and then into northern China. Eventually, it was the descendants of this group that populated the Americas.

Major genetic markers of the M130 line (part of the C haplogroup) are the ones who with perhaps as few as 500 or 1,000 people left Africa and, traveling about 4 Km per year along the seashores, eventually arrived in Australia about 60,000 BCE. Some of this group, now probably swelled in number to many more and having overcome disease and incredible travails, split off and went northward. These initially populated Japan and eastern China.

Another group of OOAs, identified as M173 haplogroup, having established themselves in western Asia, moved by unknown pressures, and began to migrate farther westward. This group eventually entered Europe, and encountering harsh weather conditions because of glaciations, swung south toward Spain, North Italy, and the Balkans.[56] These are now, perhaps because of the selection pressure of the environment, identified as M173—they were the people we call Cro-Magnon and were fully modern humans. It is at this time, some 35,000 BCE, that fully modern art appears, indicating that a new people, with a greater ability level than the Neanderthals they displaced, had arrived. This is the era of the cave art in southern France. What language they spoke we do not know. This map, copied from the Genographica site with emphasis added, shows all major human movements as of 20,000 to 15,000 BCE.

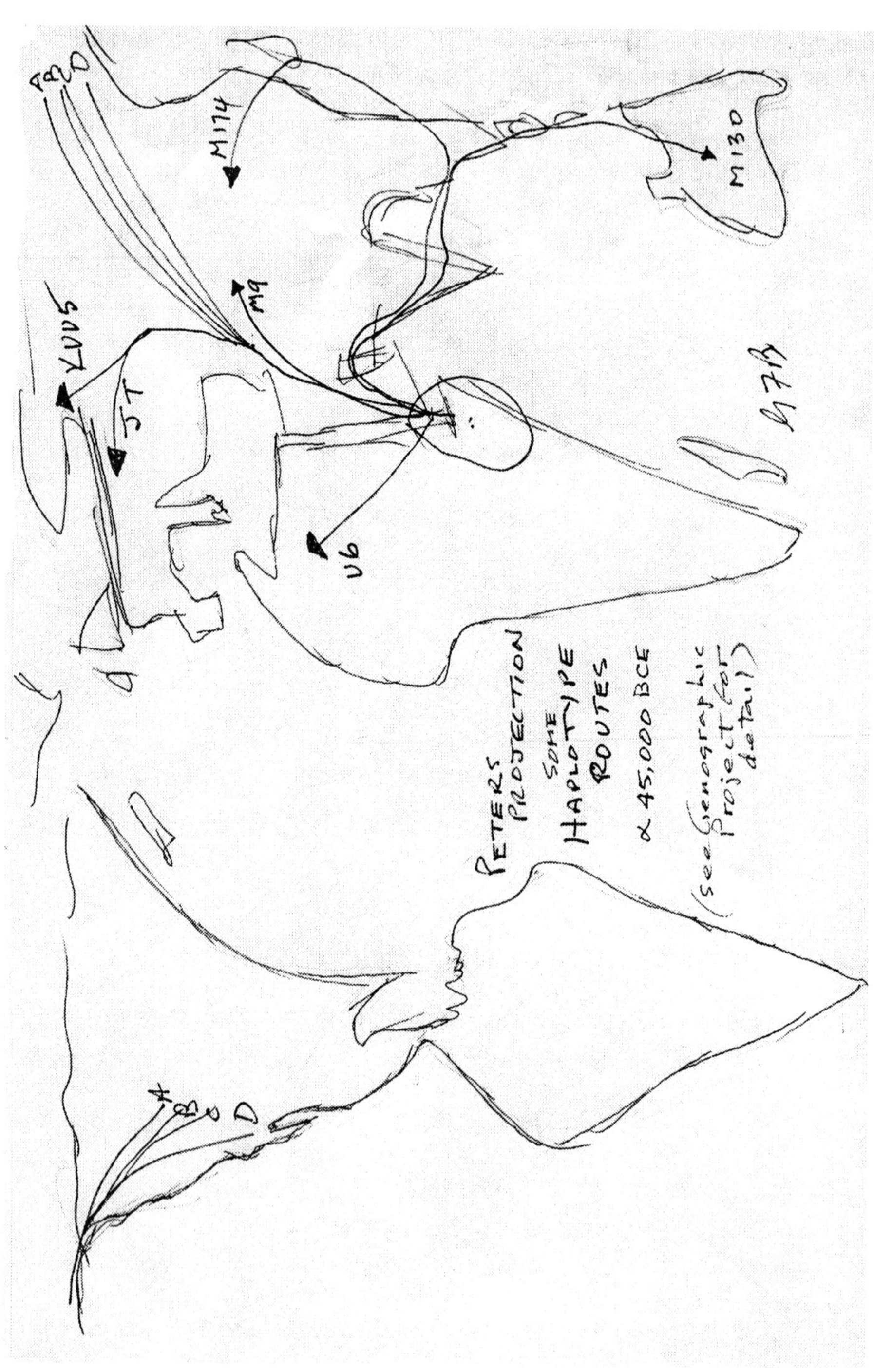
M174
M130
M9
JT
U6
PETERS PROJECTION
SOME
HAPLOTYPE
ROUTES
c 45,000 BCE
(see Genographic Project for detail)

It also shows, by my emphasis on the map, the travels of the various haplotype groups: M173 and M343, in Europe; and the M130 group, that populated Australia, Japan and China; and ONE element of haplotypes representing those of A, B, C, D, and X in their moves into the Americas. Also shown are the glaciations that covered much of Europe and the northern regions of the planet. You may be able to follow other genetic markers on the map as well.

Interesting for us, some of the groups that left Africa went into northern India, first entering Asia and then moving south into Northern India. They eventually reentered Asia and spread throughout the area north of the Caspian Sea and into Europe where they founded the line of Indo-Europeans, about whom there was reference in Chapter 1.

The Neanderthals apparently entered western Asia as an offshoot of very early HOMO ERECTUS. However, some remains have been found in Spain and in Israel (Mt. Carmel), but none in Africa proper, consequently the exact origin of the Neanderthals remains unclear. Evidence of these modern-looking, though heavy-boned and browed people, is found only in western Asia and Europe, where they left minimal traces and were eventually displaced completely from the record, probably by HOMO SAPIENS by about 30–35K BCE.[57] No evidence, even after many investigations, can be found of any interbreeding between Neanderthals and HOMO SAPIENS.

Another group of Homo Sapiens, those with a sub-group of the C-haplotype, were of two orders. One, which probably did not have proper developed speech patterns and therefore was not able to communicate well, entered Europe and Asia about 150,000 BCE, and moved about, but left few traces and evidence suggest was not fully sentient.

Yet, another group of HOMO SAPIENS, coming along later, at about 75,000 BCE had achieved proper speech in Africa through; it is tentatively established that a genetic change enabled speech development. This change in a gene, now labeled FOXP2, distinguishes those who cannot make the sounds of proper speech, despite otherwise appearing and acting "normally." To this day, this gene, if missing, does not permit the formation of proper grammar and speech, even in modern families; consequently, it is supposed to enable speech in those with the gene. So, many years after the first human began to speak, somewhere in Africa, there were several more, and then more and more, as the seminal group expanded and used its communication capabilities to make rapid progress in all areas of human activity—a clear example of evolutionary selection.[58]

Archaeologists have noted that the gap of some 75,000 years between the arrival of these speaking humans and their precursor HOMO SAPIENS at about 150,000 BCE is devoid of evidences of artistic and other truly human activities.[59] It is about 75,000 BCE that the first evidences of art, jewelry and delicate fabrications were detected. It is surmised that the bleak years—the 75,000 year period devoid of evidences of any artistic themes—reflect the absence of proper speech ability and, therefore, a minimal ability to pass on findings except by direct observation.

Language made great improvements in humanity's conditions possible. It provided a swift means of learning; it made possible the transmission of techniques and tales over large areas and time spans; it improved the efficiency of the exchange of goods and of ideas; and created among the group or tribe the ability to exchange views about the cosmos and the wonders and fears of all. An Appendix deals with the spread of language.

A recent review of a book by Professor Mithen (see note 4) attempts to describe the conditions in the days after speech developed as follows (taken from a review):

> *Before the end of the Upper Paleolithic, the world endured the last major ice advance, which peaked around 22,000 years ago at the Last Glacial Maximum. It is in those trying times that Mithen begins his history, documenting how our ancestors managed to survive—and even prosper—and setting the stage for the rapid cultural developments that followed the end of the Ice Age nearly 12,000 years ago. At that point, around the time of the transition from the Pleistocene to the Holocene (the present stage), a rapid warming began the shift toward modern climatic conditions. Farming, towns and civilizations originated over the next 5,000 years. By 5000 B.C., Mithen tells us, "the foundations of the modern world had been laid and nothing that came after—classical Greece, the Industrial Revolution, the atomic age, the Internet—has ever matched the significance of those developments.*

So, it is likely that the beginnings of the solidification of group themes and ideas were expressed through the symbolism of dance and drum before the advent of proper speech. Then grunts, shouts, mouthings and, perhaps, simple words had to suffice for communication. There is a clear thread between the ancients and the moderns via a similar means of expression—dance and music.

All of these movements of population, perhaps a maximum of 50,000 people and possibly as few as 5,000 at the start of the HOMO SAPIENS expansion, took place over a very long time with small groups stopping along the way as these hunter-gatherers moved about the countryside. These groups were subjected to the many vagaries of life, sometimes increasing in number and sometimes experiencing new diseases and enduring unimaginable constraints. All were exposed to many dangers and diseases such that the total population might fluctuate from only a very few to a more robust group several thousands in number. Diseases and disasters would have diminished the populations of HOMO SAPIENS, creating bottlenecks in an evolutionary sense.

Recent research, using DNA[60] on living Asians and native North Americans points to a single small group about the size of a single tribe—say 200 to 300 people with about 70 adults of reproductive age—that crossed the exposed land at the Bering Straits and founded the first population, some 20,000–15,000 years BCE, in the North American continent. This seems correct in a limited sense and may apply to a founding population, but it surely cannot account for the several surges of inflows that are known, through similar DNA studies, to have taken place.

About 35,000–40,000 BCE some humans in various parts of the world began to use materials such as soot and ocher to memorialize their exploits through handprints and, perhaps by some rituals, including burials, which may have been developed by this time. Some of these inscriptions, or drawings, were done on sheltered, open rock faces, and some were done inside caves. What the circumstances were that induced these artistic expressions we cannot know, although they seem related to early shamanistic practices—religion perhaps. But the important thing to note is that in all of the French caves, which spread over many miles, there is the common theme of hunting game for food and venerating the results.

4

THE BRAIN, BRAIN SCANS, AND ECSTASY

Views about the Brain

The brain is wider than the sky;
For, put them side by side,
The one the other will include
With ease, and you beside.

The brain is deeper than the sea,
For, hold them, blue to blue
The one the other will absorb,
As sponges, buckets do.

The brain is just the weight of God,
For, lift them pound for pound,
And they will differ, if they do,
As syllable from sound.

—(Emily Dickinson)

This wonderfully developed and mysterious pudding-like mass inside our skulls is the seat of our emotions. It is the sole avenue through which we have an appreciation of the inner and the outer world—all that we know and can know is related to our brain. It runs thousands of the body's systems without our conscious awareness and yet is the seat of consciousness.[61] It is the "me" or "I" that replies when we are asked, "Who did that?" It senses, via sight, sound, touch, temperature and "awareness," things that may harm or please. It looks after all of the 'housekeeping' entailed in keeping us alive. It carries our short-term memory and our long-term memory. It stores, reviews and passes on impressions and words, or memories that are now called *memes*[62] For mythology, it is long term memory and memetics, the genes of culture that are important.

Long-term memory resides in the brain, but where? Now that brain imaging machines (MRIs, PET scanners, fMRI, and the like) permit humans to look at their brains at work, we may think that we really know what is going on inside our heads. Not so. As far as can be determined, the brain may have 1,000,000,000 elements called neurons; it also has about as many glial cells, long thought to have little function in thought. Each neuron has about 10,000 connections to other neurons; consequently, if one thinks about that, it can soon be realized that the total interconnections among neurons is vastly beyond comprehension. It is now known that the glial cells do, indeed, have some role to play but exactly what that role might be, is still unclear. The brain's neurons can connect with each other in a 'neural net' that can re-order itself in an instant. Thus, there are probably more connections to be made within a brain than there are atoms in the universe. It seems unlikely, however, that humans will ever be able to explain fully what is going on inside their heads.

A recent book by two psychiatrists, specialists in neurological research and brain imaging techniques,[63] describes many experiments among the Tibetans, the Indians, and others that, in conjunction with a detailed examination of the brain's neurology, make the case that ALL religious experiences originate in the human brain. As all human brains have the same basic structure, this is a clear statement that religion and the supernatural elements of religion are found universally within the human brain. Thus there is no external overarching mind or presence of God; there is only a genetically driven possibility for the ecstatic and out-of-body experiences that we (many of us) have experienced.

D'Aquili and Newberg describe the neurological and biological mechanisms involved in mystical experiences and trances—the neurophysiology of religious experiences. A number of these involve—as has been posited by ethnologists such as Campbell and Claude Levy-Strauss—the pairs of opposites such as good-evil, up-down, and Eliade' sacred and profane. The aim of the work is to construct a neurotheology and a metatheology. In this they are, I think, successful. At the very least, their work seems to place the origin of religious feelings inside our heads.

Recent ideas, derived from computer studies, suggest that the brain is, indeed, a sort of "neural net computer," perhaps with some specialized areas—a neural net with add-ons. Neural networks have been studied in an attempt to begin to understand how the human brain might function. A similarity between the computer-brain and our brain is that the network of computer relations can be trained, so that a question asked can be answered without a program to run and instruct it. The analogy to our brain is obvious—it is a learning device. It is now thought that memories are not located in any specific place in the brain. Certain specific areas seem always to be involved in the recall and the storage of memories, perhaps as centralized switching or review stations.

In summary, the brain is a physical system and analogous to a sophisticated computer; its circuits (or its ability to create networks) are mainly designed by natural selection; consciousness is hidden and most of the brain's 'housekeeping' activities are not recognized by consciousness. As most of this was developed during Paleozoic times millions and hundreds of thousands of years ago, the conclusion is that the modern mind hides a stone-age brain. What interests me most, though, is memory.

The simple view I have about the memory is that the brain is like the conductor of a symphony orchestra playing an intricate composition. Recent studies lend credence to the idea that there seem to be certain brain structures that are involved with the overall handling of information, such as sight, hearing, speech, and the general controls of the body. The neural net is the best approximation of what actually happens within the brain with regard to general information that arises from the business of living.

Impressions that flood in from outside the brain can be likened to the score of a complicated orchestral piece. A conductor, hypothesized in the brain to be an algorithm, called a General Symbolic Machine (GSM)[64], assigns parts of the incoming impressions to various areas and instruments of the "orchestra" that together produce the entire complicated sound inherent in the score.[65] To carry the analogy a little further, the GSM also has the ability (it is not a place where memories reside, it is an algorithm) to reconstitute the entire sound of the score if it is "awakened" by almost any part of the sound that is ultimately produced. Thus, a fragment of a tune will enable a human to immediately recognize (and perhaps hear) the complete composition that was produced by the whole orchestra some time ago. Although this is a tentative explanation of the way the human brain deals with memories through association, it is not likely far from a definitive explanation. Who, after all, cannot associate the smell of smoke with a cascade of associations—danger, fire, flee, etc? With its immense ability to entertain hundreds of millions of impressions gathered over an entire lifetime, the brain is awesome in the way that quick recall can be accomplished. This view of the brain indicates that whenever an element of the mystical, the ritualistic, the ethical, or the mythological is encountered, all of the previously experienced impressions are available to the consciousness. This, I clam, is the process of remembering important myths.

This concept derives from Dawkins' *The Selfish Gene* and is extended so that, in opposition to E. O. Wilson's comment that, "Genes hold culture in a leash," *memes* (culture) consisting of the important elements of song, stories, habits, skills, and myths, influence genes through evolutionary processes.

The previously mentioned *memes* have recently been the subject of much interest for their possible effect upon evolution. Professor Susan Blackmore describes *memes* as follows:

> *I call the process by which memes control gene selection "memetic drive." memes compete among themselves and evolve rapidly in some direction, and genes must respond by improving selective imitation—increasing brain size and power along the way. Successful memes thus begin dictating which genes will be most successful. The memes take hold of the leash. In a final twist, it would pay for people to mate with the most proficient imitators, because by and large, good imitators have the best survival skills. Through this effect, sexual selection, guided by memes, could have played a role in creating our big brains. By choosing the best imitator for a mate, women help propagate the genes needed to copy religious rituals, colorful clothes, singing, dancing, painting and so on (including myths). By this process, the legacy of past memetic evolution becomes embedded in the structures of our brains and we become musical, artistic and religious creatures. Our big brains are selective imitation devices built by and for the memes as much as for the genes.*[66]

Memes have recombination, imperfect copying, selection (as when their variety exceeds the support ability[67]) and heredity, which ensure that the *memes* assist the gene's reproduction and maintenance. That is, that the useful *memes* are passed on and the poorer or less useful ones are forgotten or "die." Among these useful *memes* are: stories, myths, cuisine, language and accents, songs, music, dance, belief in ghosts, and religion. One might say that genes are entangled with culture and culture with humanity.

Blackmore makes some interesting points about the ability of *memes* in the learning process. She cites 1995 experiments at Yerkes Regional Primate Center in Georgia in which similar problems were presented to chimpanzees and babies. Only the human babies readily used imitation to solve the problems. She also suggests that the well-known fact that human babies are born with smaller heads than they develop after birth is related to the acquisition of *memes* in the babies' developmental stages. She thus attributes a major utility to *memes*—assisting both in the birth (smaller heads so that birth is possible) and in the superiority of humans in cognition.

There are many who reject her use of *memes* and the strict definition of "imitation" that she uses. This word, imitation, has caused many psychologists to refute her general claim of the importance of *memes* and several critics given space in the *Scientific American* article noted that point. On the whole, I'm inclined to agree with Blackmore and see *memes* as an explanation of why myths (and religion) have remained with society *ab initio*.

BACKGROUND

But why are there such similarities among myths? Why are they so similar worldwide? Why do so many myths involve water and floods? Why the emergence from the underground? How does religion start and how do myths develop? These are the questions that this book started with. Do we have an answer? To begin, we must first examine consciousness, and our appreciation of how that, and our brain works.

Some neurobiologists and neurologists ascribe consciousness to a God-gene—a sure-fire way to attract attention but difficult to prove experimentally; some others look to basic physical elements—quantum processes, for example—to explain consciousness, memory, feelings, and qualia. Dr. Gerald Edelman's[68] book, *Wider Than the Sky*, uses theories founded in neurology and eschews quantum physics,[69] computer programming comparisons, and philosophy. Instead, he presents a difficult and, eventually, an incomplete explanation of consciousness and one that does not deal with religious explanations.

Edelman looks to brain structure as a key factor. All humans have—amazingly—nearly identical brain structures. He points out that the neurons of the brain are developed during maturation; migrate toward their 'homes'; are pruned away as the fetus develops, and continue to grow and increase in number after birth. The neurons move to, generally, specific locations and clump together to build the basic structures. These groups of neurons tend to be activated together—to fire together—and become the brain's basic operating units. Edelman speaks of re-entrant connections or patterns and paths to and between groups, so that a path from A to B is supported and enhanced by a path from B to A.

Some patterns, Edelman holds, reinforce each other, while others are changed or die out—a rather Neural Darwinism that resembles evolutionary processes. His analogy for this process is drawn from the immune system. It produces many antibodies but, when confronted by an invader, rapidly responds and may create new antibodies, perhaps some never before seen, in order to counter the invaders. Edelman's theory of neuronal group selection—called TNGS—explains how the brain can recognize objects in the world without having an immense list of patterns. My concern with Edelman's explanation of consciousness is that it seems too mechanical to explain qualia being the same in all humans (reds are red and have the same frequencies to all though perceived differently by a few) and, our interest, in religion.

A recent book, based on the work of Eugene D'Aquili and Andrew Newberg, the former (now deceased) a professor of psychiatry, the latter a doctor skilled in radiology and both of the University of Pennsylvania, makes the case that there are areas in the human brain that, when activated by relevant stimuli, produce the feelings and experiences usually ascribed to religious epiphanies and feelings of communion with the universe. Such feelings have been and are experienced by many.

The idea of a higher being is seen in many religions, and we have noted the shaman's journey to consult higher powers in earlier chapters. In the now dominant religions of the West and in Hinduism as well, the higher being is called God. In all these theistic religions, God is the ultimate, or the transcendent, and immanent. God is considered the fundamental substance of being. Nonetheless, much of the study of religion in the first half of the 20th Century was constrained by the relativistic ideas of Franz Boas. Today a significant amount of work is being done on the common core elements of human cultures and religions.

It seems that, universally, the search for God involves ritual and a rhythmic pattern of actions that take the form of prayer, dance, and story telling by groups, to reinforce the foundational myths and the mythic structure of the society.[70] Rituals may also involve individuals through contemplation, meditation and prayer.

A theology is developed by belief in the transcendent truth of the foundation or fundamental myth of the society. It is this belief that assists the development of a body of views that bolster the perceived truth of the founding myths. In Eastern religions, theology develops from an attempt to derive meaning from both the founding myths and the experiences of 'holy' men as is seen in both Hinduism and Buddhism.

Science and theology may be considered in several ways—as antagonistic (with sociobiology noted), as independent and occupying separate areas (Stephen Jay Gould's separate *magisteria*), or as areas for discussion with boundary questions (quantum theory and the big bang are insoluble matters). Other boundary questions in our lives are: trust, anxiety, and death. There is also the possibility that science and religion are aspects of the same thing and can be integrated. One such possibility is that of the Gaia theory[71]—that all things derive from the inherent order of the universe so that all elements have been designed to permit human life. The idea that science and religion have these ways of relating one to another—conflict, independence, dialogue, and integration—is the basis of much study. However, I will concentrate on the integrative possibilities.

The remainder of this book will, then, concentrate on the integration aspects of science and religion—that they are different parts of the same thing and provide an explanation of the use of the word "mystic" in the title of the book under discussion. The theology of the Christian world derives from the Bible, church traditions and rituals, and the culture of the times. In Judaism, the basis of theology is the myths, the Torah, and other writings and commentaries. For Islam, theology is based upon the Bible and the teachings of Mohammed as recalled in the Koran. The culture and language of Arabs permitted the evolution of theological studies. Both Hinduism and Buddhism have many texts and myths and both use group rituals, as in the West, but both also involve meditation as an integral part of their religion.

Consequently, we recognize both the intellectual components of religion and the rituals and practices derived in part from the cultural time in which it was developed. Group rituals and private meditation are similar in that both of these involve subjective sensations of awe, peace, tranquility or ecstasy. Again, the shaman comes to mind. Both additionally involve degrees of a unitary experience. If the processes arising from either practice is intense, there is a collapse of the distinction between the individual and the external inanimate objects and a feeling of the abolition of all boundaries—an altered state of consciousness termed absolute unitary being—AUB.

The significance of these altered states of consciousness is seen in the mystical heritage of Eastern and Western traditions alike. Hinduism and Buddhism, as well as Christianity, Judaism and Islam, all have mystical experience in their histories. Such experiences are commonly thought of as the way in which individuals can enter the presence of God. It has been established that some 40% of individuals in the USA claim to have had some mystical experiences; and 90% believe in God. Certainly mystical experiences support religion and most religions have incorporated mystical experiences into their foundational myths—for example: Moses talks to God; Mohammed enters the desert cave to hear God; and Jesus goes into the wilderness. Mysticism and meditation are the ways that individuals come to partake of the ultimate reality—the realm of God.

HOW THE BRAIN WORKS[72]

In the following section, I have drawn, mainly, on the book by D'Aquili and Newberg, "The Mystical Mind" (Fortress Press, 1999).

The brain has developed over eons of time with older parts being added to and overlain by newer parts—but there have been relatively few changes in basic structure in the time that this book deals with. Thus, as noted previously, most human brains are quite similar in structure. There are two hemispheres that contain the cerebral cortex—the place where higher-level cognitive functions, as well as the seat of sensory and motor control, are located. The cortex is also the place where our intelligence and, with its newer parts, language, art, myth, society and culture are found. The two brain hemispheres are separate but are joined by a structure called the *corpus callosum*. Various areas generally responsible for attention, vision, orientation, motor control, and sensory functions have also been located.

The specific parts of the brain seem to be organized by their overall functional characteristics. **The visual association area** alerts the person to objects of interest through interconnections with the autonomous nervous system and the limbic system.[73] And, as we shall see below, coupled with the area of the brain that helps in orienting us and the object, it allows for the object to be detected and fixated upon.

The orientation association area of the brain is able to create a three-dimensional impression of the individual and its parts in space. The ability of the brain to create an image in space and rotate it to see the other side is exceptional and obviously of evolutionary value. The ability of the body to be able to grasp an object and to realize when the object is beyond its grasp is controlled by this system.

The **attention association area** undertakes the analysis of incoming impressions or stimuli, determines a response and then acts. The outputs are assigned to primary, secondary and tertiary areas. Some stimuli—say incoming visions—are primarily dealt with by a system (the eye) that deals with shapes, lines and colors, and then these patterns are relayed to the secondary vision cortex where associations are made and an image is created. This is at the level of understanding of 'small four legged animal;' the next or tertiary association area then produces from memory, or by deduction, the final resolution—'John's dog.' The tertiary association area is linked to the emotional system by many connections with all of the secondary and tertiary association areas. This area also gives us a sense of our spatial organization and where we are in relation to others.

The verbal-conceptual association area integrates sensory inputs to the brain and maintains rich interconnections with vision, hearing, and touch areas. It is responsible for the generation of abstract concepts and linking them to words. It is involved with conceptual comparisons, the ordering of opposites, naming objects, and categories, as well as higher order grammatical and logical operations. It is also probably involved in the development of consciousness and the expression of that through language.

These are the four tertiary association areas and they assist in the formulation of myth, ritual and religion. In humans, the limbic system—the part of the brain that develops and modulates our feelings of fear, happiness, aggression, sadness and love—allows us to have complex thoughts and to assign emotional value to them.

There are four (again) parts of the limbic system that are of importance in our study of religion, myth, and ritual. They are the: Hypothalamus, thalamus, amygdala, and hippocampus, all of which are well connected within the brain to many other parts. The most ancient is the **hypothalamus**: it has both a calming and an arousal function—"fight-or-flight"—and it produces our feelings from pleasure to bliss. These feelings have a short life when the original stimulus is removed. The **amygdala** is preeminent in control and mediation of higher order emotional and motivational functions, for example, the ability to discern and express subtle emotional and social nuances of love, affection, friendliness, fear, distrust and anger. It is also involved in attention, learning, and memory. It maintains attention if something of interest occurs. Its orienting function generates a sense of religious awe that can be related to rituals such as bows, or signs that are inserted into slow ritual rhythms. The emotional tone will tend to persist over time and slowly diminish after the stimulus is encountered.

The **thalamus** is the major sensory relay system to the new or neo-cortex and can mediate in preventing emotional extremes. This ability to inhibit transfer of information from one region to another is important in generating mystical experiences. The final element is the **hippocampus.** It helps to maintain baseline functions and plays a major role in information processing memory, new learning, attention, cognitive mapping of the environment, and some orienting reactions. It interacts with the amygdala and generates emotions related to images, learning, and memory.

Another element—a concept—that is crucial to the model of the mystical state; is **deafferentiation**[74]. It is a condition wherein areas of the brain are cut-off—deafferentiated—as in epilepsy. One part of the brain becomes over-excited and a seizure spreads from one hemisphere to the other. We have seen in the section above, dealing with shamans, that seizures can be brought on through trances and other insightful actions. Functional deafferentiation occurs when inhibitory fibers from a brain structure blocks the transmission of information to a neural structure. For example—a famous one from Drs Gazzaniga[75]—when the *corpus callosum* that joins the two brain hemispheres is surgically cut, the two halves, with no communication, will make-up reasons for an action ordered by one side (through shielding the eyes to a written order) but not known to the other. There is similar evidence that such a blocking of information transmission between the two hemispheres can occur through actions of the attention association area by the inhibitory fibers of the hippocampus.

Normally any brain structure's operations are modified by connections to many other areas. An orientation area generates a sense of space and time. If deaffaerentiated, this area tries to create its sense of time and space but cannot do that and so it has a sense of no time and no space. Total deafferentiation is undoubtedly involved in generating mystical states. This can be seen via brain scans of many types. One type gives anatomical images and it lets one see what the body looks like—the other gives functional images in real time—it lets one see what the body does.

From these studies, several primary functional components of that part of the brain have been identified, that provide consciousness and deal with thought, perception, emotion, will, memory and imagination—the mind. These so called operators of the mind are specific functions that specific parts of the brain perform as a part of the mind. They—the *Cognitive Operators*—are analogous to + and - in arithmetic but deal with sensory perceptions, thoughts and emotions. Infant studies show that these cognitive operators are active in the womb and indicate programming via genes. These cognitive operators allow the mind to think, feel, experience, order and interpret the universe around the body. They are located in various parts of the brain and D'Aquili mentions all of their locations. Seven such operators have been discovered. They are:

1) *Holistic operators*—supplemented by inputs from other places, they allow one to view reality as a whole or gestalt. They allow one to apprehend the unity of God or the oneness of the universe.

2) Reductionist operators—can break down the whole into parts for analysis and is one underpinning of scientific thought. Both the holistic and the reductionist operators allow one to view and understand a total reality.

3) *Causal operators*—produce a sense of causality and sequence and are related to our ability in science, philosophy, religious speculation and belief. The causal operators and imperative has led to myth formation and religious belief. Religions generally offer an answer to why things happen in the universe—where are the power sources and, in theistic religions, where and what is God—the ultimate cause of uncaused things. However here we must guard against a common mistake—that correlation is linked to causation. Another problem is that of the relationship between determinism and religion and science. Going back in the Western tradition to Democritus and Newton it appeared that once the original conditions of the universe were set, its future was determined by the calculations embedded in the Newtonian system. That was not the case in Eastern philosophy. There the interdependence of events becomes important and determinism is more probabilistic than might appear. Thus Eastern philosophy related to causation is closer to the principles of quantum physics than to Newtonian physics. (see Appendix B for further discussion).

Yet there are questions that arise when one considers the probabilistic system developed around quantum theory. This theory, proven to a high degree of certainty through experiment, states that matter and energy have the property of both particles and waves. Yet it is possible to augment the basic theory of indeterminacy by adding non-local elements so that quantum and Newtonian theories agree and determinism appears! But doing that does not answer the question "what is reality? And what is causal?"

As D'Aquili and Newberg state with regard to the operation of the causal operator:

> *This is the only manner in which we can satisfy the causal imperative that forces us to pose the question as to why God exists. In fact we might suggest that the causal operator is crucial to our understanding of the concept of God, for if we search hard enough for causes, we eventually work our way back to a first cause that appears not to be caused by anything else. It is the first and ultimate cause that many religions call God. This conclusion alleviates our urge generated by the causal imperative.(p.54)*

4) *Abstractive operators*—permit the formation of general concepts from individual facts. For example, to place the various elements of impressions—say, golden retrievers, poodles, sheep dogs, etc—into a general category that can then be sent to the speech centers to produce the word "dog" in English (or whatever language the person uses). General concepts or ideas underlying languages are derived from the abstractive operator. In certain patients, there is an inability to use the concepts of "larger than" or "farther than," and "better than," etc, if parts of the left hemisphere are damaged.

5) *Binary operator*—forms dyads and opposites and permits the abstraction of meaning from the external world. This element is of particular importance in generating myth. The dynamics of myth almost always involve the resolution of conflicts in the form of dyads—good, evil—and the presence of Gods and demons, who bring the opposites together in a resolution. Myths explain how good things happen to bad people and bad things happen to good people. And myths sometimes—as in Hinduism and Buddhism—involve the notion that opposites are illusions (see the Appendix, "A Universal View of the Cosmos") and that reality itself is an illusion.

6) *Quantitative operator—this* element extracts quantity from perception of various elements. It quantifies time, distance, and counting elements. It has permit-

ted the development of mathematics, measurement, and time passage—all elements of many religions.

7) *Emotional Value operator*—assigns emotional value to various elements of perception and cognition. It is important in culture, society and belief systems. While the other operators provide ways of ordering the universe and allow us to infer cause, quantity or unity in the elements or to order them in dyads, they do not incorporate an emotional value to all the other elements. The emotional value operator must be tied into all of the other operators. When it tells all about the emotional value of a matter we can act.

That is a scaled down explanation of how the brain deals with incoming sensory material. It is by no means complete and readers must consult the basic books to expand their understanding. What I hope the explanation does is allow you to recall that much of the earlier chapters in the book have resonance here—the bits about shamans and dyads, for example.

I will now jump way ahead and offer some conclusions about mysticism, ritual, ethics and myth—the same topics that this book started examining, but this time from a different perspective.

AN INTEGRATED APPROACH TO RELIGION AND REALITY

I have described AUB—absolute unitary being—as a state of the mind in which a person feels one with the universe and the higher powers, without a sense of time, or of space, and an absence of the self-other perception. A sense of pure awareness without content is achieved by certain mystics. It can also be induced by means other than introspection and contemplation of philosophical questions such as chemicals and various herbs used in religious ceremonies—mescaline, for example, and probably by the early shamans.

D'Aquili and Newberg and associates have done functional brain scans of Tibetan monks, Indian mystics, and Roman Catholic nuns while they were seeking and experiencing AUB[76] Their conclusion is that AUB is an essential component of what is called religion. Many religious leaders have experienced such a state and even more have experienced a "near death" experience and can testify about that and the feelings generated. It is, indeed, like an AUB experience and can have an affect on the individual for a long time afterwards. These leaders have communicated their general experiences to others and they, in turn, strive to attain this state—especially if they can't adhere to the urgings and commands of those who are "admitted." Thus does a sect begin to form and develop rituals, myths, and ethics that become the heart of a new religion.

To enshrine these experiences within the tribe or group, those experiencing AUB or ecstasy or trances told their stories of their journeys to the upper or lower worlds, or recounted what had supposedly transpired, thereby creating a myth. Thus were myths begun, repeated to followers, became the founding myths of the group. The powerful memetic activity repeated and nurtured those stories, added to them or embellished them, many in terms to the opposites mentioned previously, so that they truly became the foundational myths of various tribes.

In an attempt to find explanations about the mysteries of the world experienced by humans, the element of mysticism arises within the brain. In the very early days, mystics such as shamans gained access to the elements of control and domination of groups or tribes by having ecstatic experiences and relaying to the group. whatever information that they had. From this developed the foundational structure of many of our world religions.

It is supposed that the similarities of brains worldwide made it possible for quite similar myths to be developed—some were visionaries, shamans, and herders who spoke of creation from water; some spoke of creation through emergence from the ground (the opposite of burial); and some of creation through the power of naming. In Hindu mythology, the water is supporting a senior God from whom a number of lesser Gods are born or appear. In Judaism there was water in the beginning; in Christianity it is said that in the beginning was the word; and in some religions, creation was from the sun, the most evident and dominant thing, particularly if one was near the Equator.

D'Aquili and Newberg state, *"It seems most important to consider the functioning of the brain in relation to how humans experience religion and God. We have begun to take the first steps toward this new perspective on theology. This study of neurotheology is based on how the brain and mind function in order to generate and experience myths, ritual, religious and mystical phenomena."* (pg 45)

Brain structures are responsible for certain functions such as orientation in space, the passage of time, and the generation of ideas and verbalizing as well as emotions. We can begin to describe a model for generating mystical states, rituals, culture, consciousness, and near-death experiences. This last is of interest as a widely felt mystical experience and is generally described as a feeling of being outside one's body, a sensation of sliding down a long tunnel, and the appearance of a bright light at the end of that tunnel. The light is sometimes described as a benevolent "being of light" who directs the person in a review of his or her life so far and ultimately prevents the person from crossing some sort of boundary that signifies death. Most people who have had a near-death experience report that it strongly influences their subsequent lives, relieving anxiety about death, and increasing their sense of purpose, as well as their sensitivity to others. This describes a mystical experience of many, including the author.

The generation of many activities of the brain leads one to see that the whole is greater than its parts. The mind deals with intangibles—thinking, logic, art, emotions—the mind is what decides and the brain deals with the elements. The question is: does the mind/brain allow us to experience the mystical or is the brain/mind necessary to the occasion. If the former, then the mind/brain is completely responsible for the mystical: if the latter then the mystical "is out there" and can be accessed by the mind/brain. While this may seem only a philosophical question, it deals with the larger question, "What is reality?"

As we all know from physics, many elements have a duality. Light has both a wave and a particle aspect and so one regards light as a composite that, under come circumstances, can be dealt with as either one or the other—and sometimes both at once. So reality is a slippery concept. We cannot say whether the mystical is generated internally or experienced as something 'out there' by the brain/mind.

A way to handle this problem of what is reality is to examine the AUB—absolute unitary being—condition. It is well documented in the mystical literature of the world's great religions, as well as by living mystics. Brain imaging studies show that the condition is generated through deafferentiation of areas of the part named *parietal lobe* of the brain. Neither during experiencing of AUB, nor on recollecting it, have subjects ever perceived this state as subjective. It seems to be the only state to which humans have access that eludes the categories 'subjectivity' or 'objectivity.

If AUB is regarded as reality, then although neither subjective nor objective, it can be said to be generated by a specific area of the brain—the deafferentiated area of the parietal lobes. If AUB or pure subjective awareness is given priority then one must conclude that pure awareness represents reality. As counter intuitive as it seems, this requires us to believe that both individual subjective awareness and external material reality must derive from pure awareness. There may be an "out there" out there!

The self, then, has no 'a priori' status but is a practical construct arising from physical evolution. How the self may have arisen is beyond this presentation and will not be examined. Nonetheless, it is clear that certain brain structures must have developed or evolved before a conscious self could be constructed. From the perspective of the external material world, the conscious is a construct of evolutionary processes; is always aware of the 'other'; and is distinct from AUB.

A PARTIAL CONCLUSION

I have just about come full circle in this investigation and explanation of how religion is formed, what it consists of, and how the human mind produces a sensation of religion. Coupled with the actions of humans in the dim past, there developed, first, explanations of mysteries that were provided by individuals—shamans, or medicine men. From their reports, myths developed that supported the basic ideas provided by the shamans. The genetic framework of interactions with other people produced an ethical basis for groups to exist. The activities of the mind/brain permitted a variety of what we call religion to spring from the mental actions.

This, I claim, shows that many religions have the same basic origins; are all equally valid no matter what their practices; and all have elements of ritual and myth.

It also appears to me that the basics of each religion, when confined in practice to a cohesive group, are relatively benign. When several groups meet, religion is most likely to cause a conflict because each religion attacks the foundational myths of the other society.

ENDNOTES

PREFACE

[1] A search of Google shows some 7,000,000 entries showing the interest in this new field.

[2] E.W. & P.T. Barber, "When They Severed Earth From Sky: How the human mind shapes myth". 2004, Princeton University Press.

[3] This concept is mentioned by Freud and Claude Levy-Strauss and more recently by d'Aquili and Newberg and many other researchers. See S. Freud, Three Essays on the Theory of Sexuality, (1905) and d'Aquili and Newberg, The Mystical Mind," page 88.

[4] Professor Roger D. Masters. His posting to Evolutionary Psychology, which he permits me to quote, states," I'm a bit puzzled by this discussion because I know someone who developed a very different view of religion based on concrete anthropological and historical evidence (albeit primarily in Western civilization) concerning the origin and evolution of human religion. The argument, which is based on the hypothesis that natural selection (or increased reproductive success) can help explain the widespread adoption of cultural beliefs, is as follows:

"In most preliterate societies, religion plays an important part—indeed, far more important than in civilized societies. Typically, there are gods or fetishes that are associated with the lineage, clan, and or tribe. One characteristic is that this "god" or divinity protects the kin group and will do so in the future if AND ONLY IF obeyed at present. The gods are thus symbols of patriarchaldominCi!1ce over the kin group, and religious belief and practice serve to enhance each believer's inclusive fitness.-

As a result, the belief system could be viewed as a crude symbolization of kin-selected benefits of inclusive fitness in societies that lack governments uniting diverse kin groups. That is, it doesn't seem that much more is needed for an evolutionary explanation of the ORIGIN of religion than:

* development of verbal language,

* cooperation among larger kin groups than the nuclear family

* competition for valuable collective goods (such as land and natural resources) with other comparable kin groups, so that losers will encounter a relative loss in net inclusive fitness compared to winners.

* emergence of a symbolic belief to warn those who might be tempted to defect from cooperative behavior with second cousins, etc. that they run the risk of divine punishment if they defect.

* use of cultural symbols to distinguish between in-group and out-group, providing an easy way to identify outsiders (and to direct aggressive violence toward them if they are thought to be hostile).

The expansion of cooperation to level of clan, tribe, and ultimately to an alliance of tribes is especially in need of such linguistic or artistic symbols of how obedience to the rules of an "ethnic" population have the support of the unseen dominant force called one or more "gods." That is, submission to human rulers (often from one of a number of cooperating clans or tribes) is reinforced by a shared religion, according to which submission to the gods or god is submission to a dominant figure who guarantees lasting benefits to associated individuals who are only weakly linked by genetic similarity but in competition with other groups. Thus religion provides enforcement of norms that create goods shared by diverse kin groups within the tribe or "nation" which competes with comparable outside tribes or nations (i.e., groups like the "Mohawk," "Cherokee," or "Cree" Native American communities).,! This obedience to the Gods or God in a large community becomes a symbol of group-selected increases in inclusive fitness that arise from cooperation in a population larger than the primitive tribe.

\E.OWilson recently described and gave a formal definition of the rare circumstances (he called it a "bottleneck") in \ which such group selection arises. Note that at first, these larger groups—exemplified by Native American "Nations" composed of different tribes—rely on shared religious and cultural belief rather than a centralized, i bureaucracy for coordination (in good part because most activities do not entail cooperation of all members of ~each "nation" or cultural group). Ultimately, the emergence of a state composed of diverse clans or ethnic goups has a particularly strong need for symbols of the collective benefits (common good) gained from obeying powerful individuals or groups not in the clan of most residents. That's why, until the rise of the modern "nation-state," religion was typically important at the foundation of central governments with bureaucratic structures to enforce and interpret law and collect revenues. In some examples of this stage of history, the ruler of the state and the God of the religion were the same human being (as occurred with the Egyptian Pharoah who was worshipped as god). In others, as in the "Church of England," there were close institutional links between rulers and higher clergy.

[5] Boyer, P. Religion Explained: The Evolutionary Origins of Religious Thought,(Basic Books, 2001)

[6] Joseph Campbell, *The Masks of God*; VoL l, "Primitive Mythology," p. 339–342. Penguin, 1969.

CHAPTER 1

[7] J.M. Adams and H. Faure, A Review and Atlas of Paleovegitation. Quaternary Environments Network, Oak Ridge National Laboratory and Universite d'Aix-Marseilles,. Www.esd.ornl.gov/projects/qen/nerc130k.html

[8] *The Skeptic*, Vol. 24, No. 4, Summer 2005. See: www.onlineopinion.com.au/view.asp?article=3252

[9] Sir James G. Frazer, *The Golden Bough, A Study in Magic and Religion*, Collier, Abridged Edition, 1922.

[10] P. Boyer, *Religion Explained*, p.327, 328.

[11] Support for this view comes from recent findings in Journal of Neurology, Neurosurgery and Psychiatry 75 (2004) Religiosity is associated with the hippocampal, but not amygdal, volumes in patients with refractory epilepsy. See also page 29 of this text.

[12] The Skeptic, op.cit.

[13] *The Skeptic*, Vol. 24, No. 4, Summer 2005. See: www.onlineopinion.com.au/view.asp?article=3252

[14] Sir James G. Frazer, *The Golden Bough, A Study in Magic and Religion*, Collier, Abridged Edition, 1922.

[15] P. Boyer, *Religion Explained*, p.327, 328.

[16] Elaide. M, Shamanism: Archaic Techniques of Ecstasy, Princeton, Princeton University Press, 1964–2004Ed, P 23–32

[17] E. liade, M, The Sacred and the Profane: The Nature of Religion, Bollingen, 1972, P 47

[18] M. Eliade, *The Sacred and the Profane: The Nature of Religion*, Bollingen, 1972.

[19] 17 Joseph Campbell, *Historical Atlas of World Mythology*, in 4 Quarto Volumes. This work was not completed prior to his death. and A.R. Radcliffe-Brown, *The Andaman Islanders*, Ch IV, Cambridge U. Press, 1933—available on internet.

[20] Radcliffe-Brown. A.R., The Andaman Islanders, Cambridge Universsity Press, 1933 or, on internet www.sacredtexts.com/asia/tai/tai04.htm accessed 1/12/06. and Joseph Campbell, Historical Atylas of World Mythology, 4 Vo, Quarto. Uncompketed prior to his death.

[21] Mary Kingsley, "Travels in West Africa," 1897. on http://etext.library.adelaide.edu.au/k/kingsley_m/west/west.htnl (accessed 6/19/2005)

[22] To follow the ideas of the Barbers referenced in the Preface, this extinguishing of the sum MAY have been caused by a volcanic explosion or by the aftermath of an impact of a comet to the west of the area. This is sheer supposition as no dating is available.

[23] A computer search shows that flood stories or myths are worldwide and are seen in all continents and in most country mythology.

[24] Marija Gimbutas, "The Civilization of the Goddess, The World of Old Europe," Harper San Francisco, a division of Harper Collins, 1991, p.324.

[25] Frazer, op.cit, Ch LIX, p.680

[26] Frazer, op. cit. Chapter LIX

[27] World Values Survey, University of Michigan, 2005

[28] Frazer, op.cit. ChapterLIX, p.680

CHAPTER 2

[29] There is an explanation of memes below but readers are urged to look at the explanation given by Daniel C. Dennett in *Darwin's Dangerous Idea: Evolution and the Meaning of Life,* Simon and Schuster, 1995, pp. 342–373. Other references are given below.

[30] This is not intended to be a text on genetics so I provide only a simple explanation of how replication works. Some DVDs, available from the Howard Hughes Medical Institute, show the process in real time.

[31] Ursula Goodenough, "The Sacred Depths of Nature," makes this same point. She is a cell biologist.

[32] This report appeared in the *Washington Post,* May 3, 2004, Science, p. A-8. Tables of survival rates are given.

[33] An article noted in Scientific American, April 2006, P34. states that bullying triggers increased gene expression within a brain circuit linked with feelings of reward and desire. See also Science, February 10, 2006.

[34] Ayala, F.J. "The Myth of Eve," *Science 270:1930–36.* A report on research appeared in *The Times* of London on April 19, 2000, "How Seven Women Founded Europe," stated that an analysis of mitochondrial DNA (mtDNA) from 6,000 European women studies indicate that all Europeans are descended from three clans that exist in Africa today.

[35] A glance through Google will turn up many other definitions than the composite one given here. For example, evolutionary psychology focuses on the evolved properties of the nervous system, particularly those of humans. Because all tissue in living organisms is functionally organized and because this organization is the product of evolution by natural selection, a major presumption of EP is that the brain, too, is functionally organized and best understood in an evolutionary perspective. www.anth.ucsb.edu. See also L. Cosmides U& J. Tooby, "Evolutionary Psychology, a Primer," Center for Evolutionary Psychology, University of California, Santa Barbara.

[36] This section is based upon: *Humane Studies Review*, Vol. 13, No. 1: George Mason Institute of Human Studies; … Evolutionary Psychology and the Social Sciences, Tod Zywiki. See also: 'Leda Cosmides & John Tooby, *Evolutionary Psychology, a Primer*, Center for Evolutionary Psychology, UC Santa Barbara.

[37] F. Salter, "On Genetic Interests," 2003, Peter Lang, in *Nations and Nationalism*, w2005, Vol11, pg, 163–165, Blackwell. Altruism outside of kin relations may be called "good neighbor" actions.

[38] Similarities have been seen in eastern and western views about nature and man's relation to it. Appendix A—A universal View of the Cosmos—makes this clear.

[39] Giordano Bruno, a priest, was burned at the stake in 1600 for questioning the view that the world was not the center of the universe and that there might be a multiplicity of other worlds—ideas that are in the forefront of physics today.

[40] A copy of the original paper is appended as Appendix A. It may be seen as the start of a Second Enlightenment.

[41] A devastating critique of the traditional view of human nature is to be found in Tooby, J and Cosmides, L (1992), "*The Psychological Foundations of Culture*," in Barkow, J and Cosmides, L and Tooby, J, "The Adapted Mind," Oxford University Press, Ch 1, pp 19–136.

[42] Genes actually regulate the production of proteins. Each protein assumes various folded shapes that seem to almost determine its functions. Genes can produce many proteins and each protein may have many uses depending on which chemical signals trip it into action. Thus there are myriad more proteins than there are genes. Not much is known about this.

[43] Supporting the new "sociobiology" and the genetic approach of Dawkins were Maynard Smith, a leading evolutionary biologist who died in 2004; W.D. Hamiiton, who developed a rigorous basis for the existence of kin selection; and George Williams, in the USA at Stoney Brook. Opposing the new Darwinian interpretations were Steven Rose, a neurobiologist whose recent book *The 21st Century Brain* contains a continuing criticism of evolutionary psychology; Richard Lewontin; Leon Kamin, an author with others of *Not in Our Genes*, and Stephen J, Gould, who differed (he died in 2002) mainly in emphasis with Dawkins. It seems that the growing evidence for a perhaps softer Darwinism than

espoused by Dawkins is winning the day. The debate continues. My own view is that humans have the ability to override genetically imposed drives—for a time.

[44] S. Pinker, *The Blank Slate: The Modern Denial of Human Nature,* Viking, 2002. The material below relies greatly on this book.

[45] Connectionism or the concept of the neural network is interesting but a concept difficult to replicate on any meaningful scale. A gene is like an "if/then" statement so that a gene does not code for a specific protein but has the opportunity, influenced by body chemicals, to have the protein become a cell in a specific place in a growing body. There are many genes and each can code for many proteins. Neuron pathways, from their beginning to their eventual place in the brain, are only somewhat understood. See, "Language, Biology and the Mind," a talk with Gary Marcus, Edge 133. January 28, 2004, <www.edge.org>

[46] See in particular Michael Gazzaniga, "The Split Brain," *Scientific American,* 1998, also "The Social Brain," Basic Books 1969,

[47] Pinker, S, *The Blank Slate: The Modern Denial of Human Nature,* p.57. There is also a chart.

[48] Brown, Donald, *Human Universals,* McGraw Hill, 2000

[49] J. Campbell, op.cit., pg 44–47

[50] Campbell, op. cit., p. 141. and J.E. Cirlot *A Dictionary of Symbols,* Barnes and Noble, 1971.

CHAPTER 3

[51] Adams, J.M. and Faure, H.A., A Review and Atlas of Paaleovegetation(Quarternary Environment Network,. oak ridge National Laboratory and Universite d'Aix-Marseilles) www.esd.ornl.gov/projects/qen/nerc130k.html acacessed December 20, 2006

[52] Four types of humanoids, Paranthropus Boisei, Homo Rudolfiensis, Homo Habilis, and Homo Ergaster, tHomo Erectus first with tHomo Erectus essentially modern body form, all lived in Kenya about 4 ½ million years ago. *Scientific American,* January 2000, p.61.

[53] Dawkins, R., *The Ancestor's Tale*, Houghton Mifflin, 2004. p. 84. What follows related to migrations is based on P.A. Underhill, *Cold Spring Harbor Symposium on Quantitative Biology*, Vol. LXVIII, 2003, Cold Spring Harbor Laboratory Press, "Inferring Human History : Clues From Y-Chromosome Haplotypes"

[54] Other DNA studies are based on female—mitochondrial—elements that also do not change and offer information about ancestry.

[55] A new effort to track humanity's movements is underway by *National Geographic* magazine, with assistance from IBM and another foundation. Interesting maps may be seen at <www5.nationalgeographic.com/genographic/atlas.html> NOTE: the word GENOGRAPHIC! I urge all readers to look at these maps. They do not show the exact movement described above, probably because of differing or more complete sources and analysis, and are unclear in reproduction. One of the maps is reproduced here. See also the *National Geographic* of March 2006 that has some illustrations.

[56] Climate changes over the past 150,000 years in Europe can be reviewed at <www.esd.oml.gov/projects/gen/nercEUROPE.html>

[57] Joseph Campbell, op. cit. notes some arrangements of bear skulls, which he calls altars, were found in southern France. The bear cult is also found in other parts of the world, including Siberia and Japan, though how these artifacts got there is a mystery—they did not travel with HOMO ERECTUS. Campbell implies that these are evidences of a sort of religion. The bear cult was alive and flourishing as late as the 1900s in parts of Asia and among the Ainu of Japan.

[58] This does not overcome the 'origin' problem—to whom did the first speaker speak? Well, the beginning of proper speech was halting and the attempts were probably copied by many—so, they settled rather quickly on a set of sound-to-idea concepts. Everyone must remember that many changes take a LONG time.

[59] That is the usual explanation but it is now noted [*Scientific American*, June, 2005, "The Morning of the Modern Mind," by Kate Wong, p 86ff] that recent findings of stone blades (510,000 BCE), the use [285,000 BCE] and throwing spears [400,000 BCE] at various places calls into question many ideas about the past. Perhaps sentience also evolved more quickly than had been supposed

60 Reported in *Science News* www.sciencenews.org/articles/20050528/fob1.aspand Bower. Bruce, "Founding Fathers: New2 World Was Settled by a Small Tribe", Science News 167, No 22, May 28, 2005—accessed February 2006

CHAPTER 4

61 Gerald Edelman, *Wider Than the Sky, The Phenomenal Gift of Consciousness*, 2004. He won the Nobel Prize for Psychology or Medicine in 1972.

62 This word was coined by Richard Dawkins in his book *The Selfish Gene*, and then used generally to refer to the cultural transmission of ideas. Daniel Dennett's, *Darwin's Dangerous Idea* has an extended explanation but see below.

63 *The Mystical Mind—Probing the Biology of Religious Experience*, Eugene D'Aquili and Andrew B. Newberg. Theology and the Sciences Series, Fortress Press, Minneapolis, 1999. They also wrote *Why God Won't Go Away*, (with Vince Raus) stating that our brains are biologically programmed to seek a god.

64 Thomas E. Dickens, "General Symbolic Machine: The First Stage in the Evolution of Symbolic Communications" *Evolutionary Psychology*, Vol. 1, 191–209. A quotation will provide some background: "The putative GSM is odd because it is a module that enables symbols to be formed and as such has no content, merely algorithms or processes. Symbols have the adaptive advantages suggested above, but there is no sense that symbols were put there in the world to provide a selection pressure and in turn create a module with internal and vertical representations of the symbols in the world. Instead, as we are discussing the selection of a process, the GSM could only be a form of computation module. This means that the GSM is an inference machine of sorts, a hypothesis imposition device that looks for symbols (equivalence) relations that might be of use in order to further reduce prior uncertainty. Thus under this model, a GSM running on stimulus equivalence principles sets up the symbolic relation as a hypothesis and this is subsequently tested."

65 The Howard Hughes Medical institute holds seminars for young people at the end of each year. One of their tapes, "Senses and Sensibilities, Part 2" contains a depiction of the neural effects of hearing a Bach Cantata—it is amazing.

66 Susan Blackmore, "The Power of Memes," *Scientific American*, October, 2000. p. 63. and *The Meme Machine*, Oxford University Press, 1999.

[67] The ability of the brain to remember material is not known; what is known is that many have been able to recite the entire Koran, the Ramayana, Norse legends and the Bible so that myths may be passed along with minor changes as if they had been memorized which, in the case of the Odyssey, may be correct.

[68] Gerald Edelman received the Nobel Prize in Physiology or Medicine in 1972. QUALIA—subjective sensations—is a difficult topic. Self and qualia seem to be two sides of the same thing as one cannot have qualia without a being to experience the sensations. See the Reith Lectures of the BBC of 2003 where Professor V.S, Ramchanandran, Director of the Center for Brain and Cognition, University of California, San Siego. These lectures may be accessed at <www2.bbc.co.uk/radio4/reith2003/lecturer.shtml> in particular Lecture 4.

[69] Roger Penrose, a well known physicist, has written *The Large, the Small, and the Human Mind,* in which he ascribes quantum processes to the neurons of the brain.

[70] Sufi dancers, Whirling Dervishes, come to mind as do the flagellants in Spain and in some Moslem areas and the rocking motions of Jewish people at the Wall.

[71] James lovelock published the idea that all aspects of the world were organized to support life and were self balancing. This view is currently to be seen in Paul Davies,"The Goldilocks Enigma; Why the Universe is Just Right for Life", Cambridge, Allen Lane, 2006.

[72] In this section of text I draw mainly on the books of d'Aquila and Newberg. Steven Pinker has written an important book, *How the Mind Works,* which brings a wealth of information about the major elements of the operations within our heads. He does not deal with what follows.

[73] The limbic system is a group of interconnected deep brain structures, common to all mammals, and involved in olfaction, emotion, motivation, behavior, and various autonomic functions.

[74] The brain also has inhibitory circuits that are different from this shutting-down of whole areas. We are inhibited from needlessly killing others by those sorts of circuits that draw upon the social background—learned inhibitions, if you will. Deafferentiation may also occur via drugs.

[75] M. S. Gazzaniga and J. E. LeDoux, *The Integrated Mind,* Plenum Press, NY, 1978

[76] The scans that give real time functional information are single photon emission tomography (SPECT) and single emission photon tomography (PET). More descriptive information can be found in :Andrew Newberg and Robert Waldman, "Why We Believe What We Believe", Free Press, 2006.

APPENDIX A

A SEMINAL PAPER BY CRICK AND WATSON

A structure for Deoxyribose Nucleic Acid
2 April 1953
MOLECULAR STRUCTURE OF NUCLEIC ACIDS

We wish to suggest a structure for the salt of deoxyribose nucleic acid (D.N.A.). This structure has novel features which are of considerable biological interest.

A structure for nucleic acid has already been proposed by Pauling and Corey (1). They kindly made their manuscript available to us in advance of publication. Their model consists of three intertwined chains, with the phosphates near the fibre axis, and the bases on the outside. In our opinion, this structure is unsatisfactory for two reasons: (1) We believe that the material which gives the X-ray diagrams is the salt, not the free acid. Without the acidic hydrogen atoms it is not clear what forces would hold the structure together, especially as the negatively charged phosphates near the axis will repel each other. (2) Some of the van der Waals distances appear to be too small.

Another three-chain structure has also been suggested by Fraser (in the press). In his model the phosphates are on the outside and the bases on the inside, linked together by hydrogen bonds. This structure as described is rather ill-defined, and for this reason we shall not comment on it.

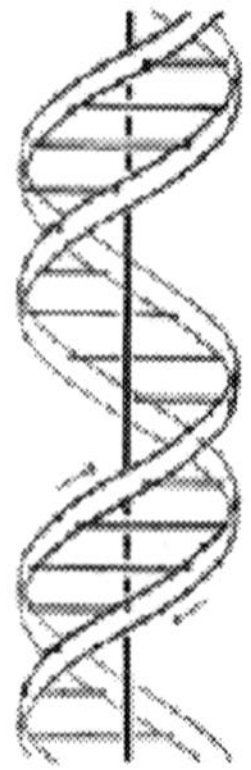

Figure 1

This figure is purely diagrammatic. The two ribbons symbolize the two phophate-sugar chains, and the horizonal rods the pairs of bases holding the chains together. The vertical line marks the fibre axis.

We wish to put forward a radically different structure for the salt of deoxyribose nucleic acid. This structure has two helical chains each coiled round the same axis (see diagram). We have made the usual chemical assumptions, namely, that each chain consists of phosphate diester groups joining ß-D-deoxyribofuranose residues with 3', 5' linkages. The two chains (but not their bases) are related by a dyad perpendicular to the fibre axis. Both chains follow right-handed helices, but owing to the dyad the sequences of the atoms in the two chains run in opposite directions. Each chain loosely resembles Furberg's (2) model No. 1; that is, the bases are on the inside of the helix and the phosphates on the outside. The configuration of the sugar and the atoms near it is close to Furberg's 'standard configuration', the sugar being roughly perpendicular to the attached base. There is a residue on each every 3.4 A. in the z-direction. We have assumed an angle of 36° between adjacent residues in the same chain, so that the structure repeats after 10 residues on each chain, that is, after 34 A. The distance of a phosphorus atom from the fibre axis is 10 A. As the phosphates are on the outside, cations have easy access to them.

The structure is an open one, and its water content is rather high. At lower water contents we would expect the bases to tilt so that the structure could become more compact.

The novel feature of the structure is the manner in which the two chains are held together by the purine and pyrimidine bases. The planes of the bases are perpendicular to the fibre axis. The are joined together in pairs, a single base from the other chain, so that the two lie side by side with identical z-co-ordinates. One of the pair must be a purine and the other a pyrimidine for bonding to occur. The hydrogen bonds are made as follows : purine position 1 to pyrimidine position 1 ; purine position 6 to pyrimidine position 6.

If it is assumed that the bases only occur in the structure in the most plausible tautomeric forms (that is, with the keto rather than the enol configurations) it is found that only specific pairs of bases can bond together. These pairs are : adenine (purine) with thymine (pyrimidine), and guanine (purine) with cytosine (pyrimidine).

In other words, if an adenine forms one member of a pair, on either chain, then on these assumptions the other member must be thymine ; similarly for guanine and cytosine. The sequence of bases on a single chain does not appear to be restricted in any way. However, if only specific pairs of bases can be formed, it follows that if the sequence of bases on one chain is given, then the sequence on the other chain is automatically determined.

It has been found experimentally (3, 4) that the ratio of the amounts of adenine to thymine, and the ration of guanine to cytosine, are always bery close to unity for deoxyribose nucleic acid.

It is probably impossible to build this structure with a ribose sugar in place of the deoxyribose, as the extra oxygen atom would make too close a van der Waals contact. The previously published X-ray data (5, 6) on deoxyribose nucleic acid are insufficient for a rigorous test of our structure. So far as we can tell, it is roughly compatible with the experimental data, but it must be regarded as unproved until it has been checked against more exact results. Some of these are given in the following communications. We were not aware of the details of the results presented there when we devised our structure, which rests mainly though not entirely on published experimental data and stereochemical arguments.

It has not escaped our notice that the specific pairing we have postulated immediately suggests a possible copying mechanism for the genetic material.

Full details of the structure, including the conditions assumed in building it, together with a set of co-ordinates for the atoms, will be published elsewhere.

We are much indebted to Dr. Jerry Donohue for constant advice and criticism, especially on interatomic distances. We have also been stimulated by a knowledge of the general nature of the unpublished experimental results and ideas of Dr. M. H. F. Wilkins, Dr. R. E. Franklin and their co-workers at King's College, London. One of us (J. D. W.) has been aided by a fellowship from the National Foundation for Infantile Paralysis.

J. D. WATSON F. H. C. CRICK

Medical Research Council Unit for the Study of Molecular Structure of Biological Systems, Cavendish Laboratory, Cambridge. April 2.

1. Pauling, L., and Corey, R. B., Nature, 171, 346 (1953); Proc. U.S. Nat. Acad. Sci., 39, 84 (1953).

2. Furberg, S., Acta Chem. Scand., 6, 634 (1952).

3. Chargaff, E., for references see Zamenhof, S., Brawerman, G., and Chargaff, E., Biochim. et Biophys. Acta, 9, 402 (1952).

4. Wyatt, G. R., J. Gen. Physiol., 36, 201 (1952).

5. Astbury, W. T., Symp. Soc. Exp. Biol. 1, Nucleic Acid, 66 (Camb. Univ. Press, 1947).

6. Wilkins, M. H. F., and Randall, J. T., Biochim. et Biophys. Acta, 10, 192 (1953).

APPENDIX B

A UNIVERSAL VIEW OF THE COSMOS

A Universal View of the Cosmos

This paper will argue that mankind has reached a common basic view of the cosmos and the nature of reality by several different paths. This has happened by virtue of the unique and common brain structure of mankind. Our brains are 'hard-wired' in certain important ways and they are also organized for discrimination and categorizing and, above all, for making inferences. These properties have caused a search for, and the adoption of, a parsimonious or simple view of nature by mankind.

Through one path man has mystically and directly developed a view of the cosmos involving fundamental ideas current in the advanced physics of current times. Through another set of paths that stress monotheism and mankind's ability to know as much as God, he has arrived by halting steps and experimental science, at a view of the cosmos quite similar to that of the mystics.

Where men have been able to form opinions that satisfy their criteria of simplicity it has seemed to me to result in such satisfaction with their view of, particularly, the cosmos that they cease to further speculate. Where men have not been able to reach a satisfying and simple view of nature and the cosmos, and where men have been told that they have a special relationship with a God, they either become imprisoned within that idea or use it to free themselves from all restraint in their attempts to know as much as the Gods.

Parsimonious reality

The brain of man is an immense construction of interrelated elements—a distributed system—of some 10 to 14th neurons. The current view of these activities is somewhat as follows: (i) while various areas of the brain tend to specialize their activities, its total activity is derived from its distributed network; all parts may participate in thought to a greater or lesser extent; (ii) while parts of the brain seem to be 'hard-wired', for example for movement detection, sound reaction, etc, and while certain defensive reflexes are only reviewed by the brain after they have occurred, it is not true that there is a single place of consciousness directing a life with a singular purpose—there is no precise theory of human nature, although the outlines of one are currently being constructed; (iii) there still seems to be, in the left side of the brain, a unique area that integrates, simplifies and examines and selects from the various impressions and instructions flowing within the brain, a single belief or course of action. This interpreting is done prior to permitting speech or further action or intellectual activity.

The interpreter is in control of belief formation and makes inferences in order not to be overwhelmed by the various instructions and impressions flowing within the brain. Some of these instructions and impressions are of a contradictory nature. Experience and reinforcement (repeated instructions) firms the beliefs and allows inferences to lead to ever more complex activity.

The power of inference implies that homo sapiens sapiens—our kind—can decouple himself from his environment. The nature of the interpreter function is to create a simple view of the world. Man's capacity to accept magic results from the parsimony of the brain—a way of explaining the inexplicable. From magic, established as myth, comes religion, which is a further refining of man's view of the cosmos and nature. Ritual tends to impress these magical and mythical elements upon individuals and groups.

Man has the power to adapt to various environments and has developed a cosmology involving a parsimonious view of the universe. Moreover, reflecting the simple cosmology, there is a tendency towards monism, in the sense that reality is made of one whole. This reflects the parsimonious and selective nature of the decisions of the 'interpreter' in the brain. Taking the civilizations East and West of Mesopotamia, we can see how monism is uniquely Eastern while Mono-theism is distinctively Western.

Eastern Mysticism

There is no such thing as the importance of an individual life in the East, only the importance of the great cosmic law. The universe is an ever appearing and disappearing dream delusion, rising and falling in recurrent cycles. One plays one's part without ego over many cycles and, if one's part is done well, one can gain release from the round of reincarnation and achieve unity with the cosmos.

The day of Brahma, in India, is 4,320 million years followed by a night of similar length, when all is dissolved in the cosmic sea and another cycle begins. Brahma is the soul and inner essence of all things and cannot adequately be described; it has no beginning, is beyond what is and what is not. Its manifestation within the human soul is Atman, and the idea that Atman and Brahma are one is the essence of Hinduism:

> *That which is the finest essence—this whole world that has as its soul. That is reality. That is Atman. That art Thou.*
>
> —Chandogya Upanishad 6.9.4.

> *All actions take place in time by the interweaving of the forces of nature, but the man, lost in selfish delusion thinks that he himself is the actor*
> *But the man who knows the relation between the forces of Nature and Action, sees how some forces of Nature work on other forces of Nature, and become not their slave.*
>
> —Bhavagad Gita 3.27–28

In the Buddhist religion man has also come, perhaps via a later interpretation and refinement of Hinduism, to a similar simple view of the universe. The essence of this religion is to be "awakened" and to pass beyond the world of the usual reality and achieve Dharma and Acinta, the unthinkable, where reality appears as undivided and undifferentiated essence. The central theme of the great Buddhist writings is the unity and interrelation of all things and events, including humans.

The Chinese Taoists also conclude that there is only one reality, which underlies and unifies everything we observe.

> *There are three terms—complete, all-embracing, and the whole.*
> *These names are different, but the reality sought in them is the same—referring to The One Thing.*
>
> —Chuan Tzu, Ch. 22 (trans J. Legge)

This reality—the Tao—is the ultimate, the cosmic process in which everything is involved, a continuous flow and change. In this respect the Tao is the same as the Hindu Brahma and the Buddhist Dharma. The Taoists saw change in nature as interplay between opposites, the yin and the yang, and they came to believe that those opposites were joined and dynamically united.

> *"This is also That. That is also This. That the That and the This cease to be opposites is the very essence of the Tao. Only this essence, an axis as it were, is the center of the circle, responding to the endless changes.*
>
> —Fu Yu-Lan, A Short History of Chinese Philosophy, p.112

Enough has been written in these paragraphs to establish that Eastern mysticism was monistic. It is quite remarkable that this monistic idea was developed through introspection alone. Without the elaborate equipment of the experimental laboratories, the "physicists" of the East have come to a clear understanding of reality that is in line with the current ideas of physics that demonstrate the quantum indeterminacy of matter.

Western Practicality

There are three main strands of Western scientific thought stemming from Mesopotamia. These are the Judaic, the Greek, and the Christian. But only the Greek and the Christian religions fully developed man's capacity for wide-ranging thought that could be called science.

Judaism, however, was not inquisitive about the cosmos. Having a special nature that arose from the fact that Jews were made in God's image:

> *And God said, let us make man in our own image after our likeness: and let him have dominion over all the earth, and over every creeping thing that creepeth upon the earth.*
> *So God created man in his own image, in the image of God created He him, male and female he created them ...*
>
> —King James Bible, Genesis, V 26–7

So Jews, for thousands of years, did little in the sciences secure in the knowledge that God ruled all and that there was no need for such investigation.

But it was different in Greece. The Greeks, living with a pantheon of gods, recognized that human traits existed in heaven. They were aware of and cognizant of the power of the Gods and the supremacy of Zeus, but were not subservient to them or to Zeus. This led Greeks to inquire about Nature and the cosmos. Man's ability for mathematical invention, and his penchant for political organization which did not unduly constrain his search for simplified interpretations of the cosmos, stood him in good stead in Greece and, eventually, in the Christian West. To my mind, Tennyson, looking back over time, put the essence of man's search for knowledge into words with:

> *Yet all experience is an arch wherethrough*
> *Gleams that untravelled world whose margin fades*

Forever and forever when I move ...
And this grey spirit yearning in desire
To follow knowledge like a sinking star
Beyond the utmost bounds of human thought ..."

—Ulysses

The lack of subservience to gods in Greece, in contrast to the subservience of the peoples of Mesopotamia and Egypt to their Gods, together with the unique political organization and the scattered nature of the Greek 'polis', was responsible for a virtual explosion of thought about the cosmos and the physical world. Much of this inquiry took place in the years from 600BC to 200BC.

This intellectual activity started in the Ionian islands among the sons of wealthy seafarers. The practicality and inquisitiveness of these people resulted in the first scientific activities of man, even including the recording and timekeeping of the heavens undertaken by the Chinese, Aztecs, and Mayans.

Startlingly enough, the Greeks came close to many of the now current ideas of science. Thales of Miletus (636–546 BC) predicted a solar eclipse, taught that mountains can be thrust up from the bottom of the sea and be worn down by wind, and learned how to measure height and prove geometric theorems 300 years before Euclid. Heraclitus (535–476 BC) was closest to Eastern mysticism; he taught that there was no permanent reality, that all things carried with them their opposites, that "being" and "non-being" were part of every whole so that the only reality was "becoming"; and that man shared his soul with a universal "soul fire".

Anaximander (611–547 BC), the fires experimental scientist, determined the length of the year and of the seasons; mapped the known world and the globe and made sun-dials to tell time; believed in an infinite number of inhabited worlds, and developed a theory of how humans arose (evolved) from other animals, all of which were spontaneously generated from the mud. "Nor", says St. Augustine, "did he any more than Thales attribute the cause of all this ceaseless activity to a divine mind".

Hippocrates of Cos (460–360 BC) was the first to develop a school of practical medicine using the physical and chemical knowledge of the time; Empedocles (450 BC) did experiments with air and taught that many sorts of beings must:

> *"have been unable to beget and continue their kind. For in the case of every species that exists either craft or carnage or speed has, from the beginning of its existence protected and preserved it."*
>
> —Carl Sagan, in 'Cosmos' (quoted)

thus anticipating some of the ideas of Charles Darwin in the 1860s AD.

Plato (427–347 BC) taught that regular circular orbits of the planets were perfect because the circle was perfectly symmetrical. Symmetry is now a key concept in physics. Plato believed that the atoms of the four elements had the shapes of solids. Aristotle ((384–322 BC), Plato's student, continued to develop these ideas, enshrining both the concept of the difference between matter and mind, body and soul; and the concentric system of spheres to represent an unchanging universe. Aristotle's lack of interest in the material world and experiment obtained a strong hold on later Christian doctrine. This was made easier by the Ptolemaic (Ptolemy 200 AD) refinements that produced a concentric model of the planets which was able to forecast most of the movements of the stars and planets.

Democritus (460–370 BC), from northern Greece, also believed in the existence of many worlds; that some were inhabited; that life arose from the primeval ooze; and that nothing exists but the atoms and the void. Aristarchus (217–145 BC), whose works arte lost except by reference, taught that the planets circle the sun, anticipating by some 1,700 years Coppernicus—who referred to Aristarchus' view in his first manuscript. Thus the Ionian school represents experimentalists, the practical ones; those who believed that Nature was accessible through thought and observation.

Finally, for this material, Pythagoras of Samos (582–507 BC) invented a mechanistic and advanced mathematical school pf thought. In about 300 BC, Euclid developed the logic of geometry. This, coupled with the anti-experimental bias of the Platonists, submerged the experimental school which died out and was lost for some 2,000 years—"the mechanical arts," said Xenophon (450–555 BC), "carry a social stigma and are rightly dishonored in our cities." (quoted in Cosmos, Sagan, p.153).

In conclusion, Greek practicality and the freedom of its rich elite, and man's never-ending speculation and search for explanations of the universe and of nature, took man close to major discoveries. Had the great library at Alexandria, where many documents from many areas were stored for the use of scholars, not been ravaged in the years following the new millennium, many more discoveries might have been made. If the early Christians had not closed the Greek schools man would have almost certainly come to the calculus (Pythagorean conic sections contain the basic idea) and to a deeper understanding of evolution and to refinements of the heliocentric concept of the solar system.

However the society of the West fell into the hands of those who taught dogma and unchanging truth and who eschewed speculation. The Romans, comfortable with their Greek gods, were interested only in the practicalities of engineering and the creation of a legalistic society, not science. With the collapse of the Roman Empire, the light of knowledge in the West was almost extinguished for a thousand years. Only Platonic ideas survived.

In the early years of the new millennium the power of the Christian church depended upon its gospel of salvation and kindness among men and on its clandestine nature. With the help of Emperor Constantine, Christianity gained official recognition as a public religion through the Edict of Milan (313 AD). This status was greatly increased when Constantine converted and by the suppression of all other religions by Emperor Theodosious, baptized in 380 AD. Thereafter, says Arnold Toynbee,

> *"In Western Christendom this monstrous regime of Christian totalitarianism, imposed by force, lasted 1,300 years. The disintegration of Western Christendom at the Reformation only aggravated the evil."*
>
> —Toynbee, "Change and Habit", p 51.

The grip of the Catholic Church on the dogma of Christianity was very powerful and it seemed as if all of the energies of man in this period were diverted away from inquiry and into efforts to maintain the faith. Through secular techniques, vast cathedrals were erected and many wonderful works of art were undertaken. But nothing of importance happened in the field of science. The few leakages of ancient Greek scientific speculation were, if in opposition to the doctrines of the Church, stamped out and treated as heresy.

Islam

Meanwhile, in Mesopotamia, a new religion appeared about 700 AD—Islam. The powerful writings of the prophet Muhammad quickly, through the sword of conversion and proselytizing of a theocratic state, came to unite and dominate the Middle East, Egypt, and the shores of the Mediterranean, launching into Europe when the Iberian peninsula became Islamic and into Greece and the Balkan area. In the early years from 700 AD to the early 13 'th Century, Islamic scholars preserved many of the old Greek texts and involved themselves with mathematics and medicine. They, following the urging of the Koran to venerate knowledge, became the world's principal leaders in most fields of science. Underlying the spread of this new knowledge—in mathematics, astronomy, medicine and the preservation of much of Greek knowledge—was the view that Islamic scholars were following God's orders to view a unified universe. Until by the 14th Century, all of Europe sought Islamic science.

Then came disaster in the form of the Mongol invasions in the 14th and 15th Centuries. After putting most to the sword and destroying the libraries and seats of learning, the Mongols imposed an autocratic rule. Baghdad fell to the Mongols in 1258 and with that a dark period began. As the Mongols were converted to Islam, several dynasties came into being and, in general, divided Islam into Shi/ia and Sunni factions. These divisions reflected the groups that adhered to one or another of the followers of the Prophet.

From this shambles and the conversion to Islam of most Mongols over several hundred years, arose three new empires—the Ottoman that lasted to 1918; the Safavid from 1501 to 1722, when Iran was made from Persia; and the Mughal from 1526 until mid-19th Century. The structure of Islam during those years, under strong Caliphs as a central religious authority, reflected the need to control the population through strict imposition of Islamic law. For much of the period after the expulsion of Islam from Europe, in 1400 AD, little was done in the Islamic world about science. Islam concentrated on parsing the Koran, the holy book of God's words. Control of the religion fell into the hands of clerics largely devoted only to interpreting God's words. Even today there is little within Islam that speaks of science, as a look at the indexes of most books about Islam will show (look under technology, science, and physics for example).

One can say that the Islamic world fell under the same sort of control by clerics that Christian Catholicism experienced. Yet, the spirit of man reappeared in the West during the Reformation. A similar event has not yet seriously affected Islam, although there are several trends to be seen—fundamentalism, modernism, and generally accepted Islam.

Christianity and Science

> In its infancy the power of the Christian church depended on its gospel of salvation and kindness among men, and its clandestine nature. With the help of Emperor Constantine of Rome, Christianity gained official recognition as a public religion via the Edict of Milan (313 AD). This status vastly increased through the deathbed conversion of Constantine and the suppression of all other religions by Emperor Theodosius, who was baptized in 380 AD.

The grip of the Catholic church on the dogma of Christianity was very powerful and it seemed that all the energies of man in this period were diverted away from inquiry towards efforts to maintain the faith. Through secular techniques vast cathedrals were erected and many wonderful works of art were undertaken. But nothing of importance happened in the field of science excepting, perhaps, the work of Roger Bacon, founder of the scientific method. The few leakages of ancient Greek scientific speculation were, if in opposition to church doctrine, stamped out or treated as heresy.

Copernicus (1473–1534 AD) whose treatise on the centrality of the sun only extended Greek ideas was only published on his death. It opened speculation about the structure of the cosmos and brought into question Ptolemaic and Aristotelean ideas that had been adopted by the Church as dogma. He was not, however, free from criticism. Catholics, Calvanists (1509–1564 AD) and Lutherans (1483–1546 AD) all deride his work:

> *"People give ear to an upstart astrologer who strove to show that the earth revolves and not the heavens of the firmament, the Sun and the Moon. Whoever wishes to appear clever must devise some new system, which of all systems is of course the best. This fool wishes to reverse the entire science of astronomy; the sacred Scripture tells us that Joshua commanded the Sun to stand still, not the Earth."*
>
> —M. Luther, in "The Wayside Pulpit #37"

> *"Who will venture to place the authority of Copernicus above that of the Holy Spirit?"*
>
> —John Calvin, Durant 858

But Giordano Bruno, who may have had contact with the writings of the East, was burned at the stake in 1600 AD for holding other than dogmatic views of the universe. He said that our perception of the world is relative to the position in space that we observe it, and that there are as many possible ways of viewing the world, as there are positions, so that there is no absolute truth. He held, also, that the individual irreducible elements comprising the world—he called them 'monads'—were based on the principle or cause, or deity, manifest in both man and the world.

With the Protestant Reformation, Christian battled Christian in bloody wars and few had the chance to follow scientific investigations. Yet, because of the weakened authority of the Church and the appearance of more lenient Protestant sects, man again began to exercise his inquisitive, rationalizing traits and science was reborn with the work of Galileo in 1633. About the same time, and with some importation of Arabic/Islamic material, intellectual activity about the nature of the world began again. Francis Bacon published his views about the proper way to carry out scientific investigation through a combination of experiment and theory, so that proving theories by observation and experiment became the norm. He invented the inductive method of science.

This new burst of scientific activity was centered in England, where there were few checks upon inquiry. With the influx of the French Hugenots after 1685, and the growing attraction of England to foreigners who relished greater intellectual freedom, England benefited over the next 300 years in much the same way that American science benefited from the influx of foreigners after the 1930s. As science was a major factor in making England the world's greatest power in the mid-19th Century, so science made the United States the world's major power after the mid-20th Century.

The pervasiveness of the Aristotelian view of the cosmos was reflected in literature. If literature is a type of reflection of the general views of the times, then a rapid survey of some literary sources will serve to emphasize how views of the cosmos became publicized.

Dante's "Divine Comedy" described a purgatory, a hell, and a heaven exactly in keeping with the Church's view of Aristotelian teaching and contrary to the helio-centric concept of the solar system then being confirmed by Kepler (1571–1730 AD) and Tycho Brahe (1546–1601 AD) and others. John Milton (1608–

1674 AD), who knew of Galileo and his works wrote, referring to the nine crystal spheres of the Church's universe wrote:

Ring out ye crystal spheres,
Once bless our human ears,
If ye have power to touch our senses so.
And let your silver chime,
Move in melodious time
And let the base of Heaven's deep organ below
And with your ninefold harmony
Make up full concert to th' angelic symphony"

—"On the Morning of Christ's Nativity" 1.125

And Shakespeare, in "The Merchant of Venice", referring to the music of the spheres:

Look how the floor of heaven
Is thick with patens of bright gold
There's not the smallest orb which thou beholdest
But in his motion like an Angel sings

—Act V, Scene 1

But some of the Copernican ideas did register. This can be seen in Milton's acceptance of a new view of the cosmos told in "Paradise Lost":

What if the sun
be the center of the world?
The planet Earth, so steadfast so she seem,
Insensibly three different motions move?

—Paradise Lost Book VIII

And John Donne (1573–1631 AD) urged man to quest for the truth in his search for the true religion and, by inference, the truth about Nature ...

... on a huge hill,
Cragged and steep, Truth stands, and he that will
Reach her, about must, and about must go
And what the hill's suddenness resists, win so;
Yet strive so, that before age, death's twilight,
Thy soul rest, for none can work in that night.
To will implies decay, therefore now do.
Hard deeds, the body's pains; hard knowledge too
The mind's endeavors reach, and mysteries
Are like the Sun, dazzling, yet plain to all eyes

—Religion, I, 79–88

With experiment linked to theory through the influence of Bacon, the need to test hypotheses by observation forced science away from dogma and toward truth which, in the manner stated by Donne, would reveal Nature's mysteries.

But literature, a good barometer of the general attitudes of peoples, did not keep up with science, particularly in Great Britain. There the dirty business of experiment and classification and the penchant of wealthy gentlemen to study the classics, contained science within a small scientific community. One glimmering of the cosmological and scientific ideas being discussed can be seen in the literature of poetry and fiction in the period from the mid-1600s until Lord Tennyson began to write in the mid-1800s. While literati were mainly ignoring science, Newtonian ideas were redesigning man's understanding of Nature.

In Jonathan Swift's "Gulliver's Travels" (1726) there appears a satirical view of the mechanistic Newtonian world. Swift created "The Academy of Logado". a reference to the 1662 creation of the Royal Society and a spoof of the word 'logic', where a giant sort of computer ground out text by the chance combination of the parts of speech, a similar system used currently to translate ideographic script into computer 'bits'. The idea that knowledge could arise from chance operations, though satirical, carries with it the notion of the future place of chance or randomness in the physical world.

Alexander Pope (1688–1774 AD), that most adept and felicitous of poets, refers, in his "Essay on Man", to the "vast chain of being which from God began" and to the ordered nature of the physical world that man should not disrupt:

From Nature's chain, whatever link you strike,
Tenth or tenthousandth, breaks the chain alike.
And if each system in gradation roll
Alike essential to the amazing whole,
The least confusion but in one, not all
That system only, but the whole must fall.
Let Earth unbalanced from her orbit fly,
Planets and suns run lawless through the sky,
Let ruling Angels from their spheres be hurled,
Being on being wrecked, and world on world,
Heaven's whole foundations to their center nod,
And Nature trembles to the Throne of God:

All this dread ORDER break—and for whom? For thee?
Vile worm!—Oh madness, pride, impiety.

—Essay on Man, l.45–258

And Pope was quite comfortable with the concept, was looking behind the unexpected to find the expected Newtonian order:

All Nature is but Art, unknown to Thee:
All chance, direction, which thou canst not see;
All discord, harmony not understood:
All partial evil, universal good;
And spite of pride, in erring season's spite,
One truth is clear; whatever IS is right.

—Line 89–294

William Blake (1757–1827 AD) in his "Book of Thel" created a multi-dimensional area "like shadows in the water" that presaged much future science. Percy Shelly (1792–1822 AD) was a Platonist. He looked in his writings at both the perfect and the imperfect or ordinary world with all its difficulties, and with little to remind us that Newton's work had been published over 100 years earlier. It ought to have been known to Shelly's inquiring mind, yet he was interested, it is said, in science and technology and it is, perhaps, this atmosphere that introduced his wife, Mary, at the age of 19 to undertake to write "Frankenstein"—which has little to do with science but awakened the public in many countries to many scientific possibilities.

Not, I think, until Tennyson's "Locksley Hall, published in 1842 during the early years of the Industrial Revolution, was science and technology brought into 'respectable' literature:

When I dipped into the future as far as human eye could see,
Saw visions of the world and all the wonder that would be;
Saw the heavens filled with commerce, argosies of magic sails,
Pilots of the purple twilight, dropping down with costly bales
Heard the heavens filled with shouting, and there rained a ghastly dew
From the nations' airy navies grappling in the central blue,
Till the war drums throbbed no longer, and the battle flags were furled
In the Parliament of Man, the Federation of the World.

—Lines 121–128

But Tennyson criticizes science. "Science", he said," moves but slowly, slowly, creeping on from point to point." However science was not creeping, it was rushing forward with almost unimaginable speed.

I will not relate here the details of the progress of science as I did in the case of Greece because the information is readily available. But certain major steps should be noted. Newton's views led toward a mechanistic interpretation of Nature akin to the Aristotelean insofar as the universe was concerned. But, in 1718 Edmund Halley discovered that major stars, supposedly fixed, had altered their positions since being charted by Ptolemy. Between 1900 and 1960 the world of science produced a Second Enlightenment and nearly a unified view of the cosmos. Except in the mind of the Catholic Church, this discovery that the stars changed their positions, destroyed the Aristotelian concept of the universe—one that was truly ancient.

Then, with improved telescopes, Emmanuel Kant (1724–1804 AD) observed spiral nebulae and developed his theory of 'island universes'. Later, in 1761 and 1769, measurements of the transit of Venus produced a good estimate of the astronomical unit—the average distance of the Earth from the Sun. A few years later William Herschel, in 1783, observed the solar system and the heavens and theorized that the many nebulae contained "the chaotic materials of future suns'.

Popularizers of science such as Jules Verne (1828–1905 AD) with his "From the Earth to the Moon", "A Journey to the Center of the Earth", and other works; and H.G. Wells' ((1886–1946 AD) "The Time Machine", and "The War of the Worlds", reached the general reader and expanded his acceptance of new views of the cosmos. But not all the views of Newton and Charles Darwin (1809–1882 AD) were accepted. Darwin, particularly, whose views about the likely development of man over archaeological time—not the few years that clerics had derived from the Bible—engaged most people in consideration of the cosmos and were accepted almost entirely by the Catholic church.

Conclusion

And where is science today? It has arrived, by Baconian experiment and theory, at a view of the cosmos that is strikingly akin to that of the mystical religions. It seems agreed that 'reality' is an ever appearing and disappearing flux of energy, transformed through an infinite series of changes into virtual particles that exist and do not exist at the same time.

Current experiments show that properties of two particles distant in space can be held constant regardless of the choice of measurement applied to either. In other words the experiments show that the universe is fundamentally interconnected and inseparable. A modern astronomer-physicist, David Bohm, says, in "The Tau of Physics",

> One is led to as new notion of unbroken wholeness which denies the classical idea of analyzability of the world into separately and independently existing parts. We have reversed the usual classical notion that the independent 'elementary parts' of the world are fundamental reality, and that the various systems are merely particularly contingent forms and arrangements of those parts. Rather we say that an inseparable quantum interconnectedness of the whole universe is the fundamental reality, and that relatively independent behaving parts are merely particular and contingent forms within this whole.

Compare this to what Nagarijunaan Indian mystic, says in the same source:

> Things derive their being and nature by mutual dependence and are nothing in themselves

And, from the Mundaka Upianishad (2.2.5),

> *He on whom the sky, the earth and the atmosphere are woven and the wind, together with all life breathes, Him alone know as one and the same.*

With these quotations I think that I have made a case for the view that Western man, believing that he was made in the image of God and endowed with a special brain, set out with varying degrees of success, to plumb the depths of knowledge. The Christians, particularly those free from the constraints of churches, were able, by experiment and tested theory, to come to realizations about the cosmos and nature similar to those of Eastern man, who had used the parsimonious nature of his inferential brain to come to similar views. Thus, several thousands of years later, the western human has caught up to eastern humans in regard to man's view of the cosmos.

George Bain, May 30, 2004

APPENDIX C

THE ADVENT OF LANGUAGE

The Advent of Language

Prior to speech the only way that humans could communicate was by direct imitation and close contact. While verbal communication was limited to grunts and growls, facial expressions and touch, communication by dance or drum—rhythmical expression—was possible. It is there that we find the first the first identifiable method of human inter-communication. That this is the case one had only to Radcliffe-Brown's work on the primitive Andaman Islanders where he notes approvingly, though in Victorian terms, that the dances "express mankind's amicable joy of life through the millenniums of those first and hardest 400,000 years". Additional support for the idea that dance is important communication is to be found in the dances of the Central Australian natives, as reported in the 1800 and in the aboriginal dances of West Ceram (part of the Indonesian archipelago). Both of these instances are also to be found in Joseph Campbell's Primitive Mythology, previously cited, where his index for 'dance' contains many examples.

But it is easy to see on a generalized map, that the movement of people is related to the languages developed over time. The figure below c an be readily related to what has been noted above—Uralic and Altaic languages, based on the currently spoken Finno-Ugric languages, are found in Finland, Northern Scandinavia, parts of Russia and in Hungary and adjacent areas. Similarly the Samoyedic languages are spread across Siberia And the Arctic and eastward to Kamchatka, where traces are to be found further east into the Eskimo (Aluet) languages. I hope to show that the basic myths of these peoples have a common origin.

If one considers the African languages there can be seen a northern group of languages, Congo-Saharan and Khosian. The Khosian language started as a "click" language that is a recognizable series of guttural and glottal sounds. It is spoken to this day among widely divergent people. One, the Bushmen, who are still hunter-gatherers, was a large population throughout south-west Africa until the Dutch arrived and, through hunting them, almost extirpated them. Today the only surviving bushmen are fouind near the southern Namibian border with South Africa. The other "click" language is spoken by the Hadza tribes of Tanzania.

It seems likely that the original language of humanity was a "click" language—perhaps the first—that was developed near the Great Rift Valley in the very early days of Homo Sapiens. From there the people spread west and south as some people migrated south-west, finally reaching the coast of the Atlantic

Ocean. There are ancient caves on the old ocean margin where artifacts have been found. The migrating people finally reached the Atlantic shore in what is now Namibia, where their descendants are found today. Othere migrated from the Rift Valley to the north to today's Tanzania where their remnants—the Hadza exist today still speaking the "click" language. This view is supported by the views of the Leaky Foundation, the discoverers of the ancient humanoids in the Rift Valley.

The Out of Africa (OOA) group that entered India and that, later, broke out into the Asian plains several thousands of years later. Driven by population pressure, climate changes and, perhaps by availability of foods, this group invaded Europe leaving behind the legacy of the Indo-European languages and indelible visions of armed horsemen riding into lands where such had never before been seen. The Centaur, half man and half horse, would have been the vision engraved on the Dorians (Greeks) when this invasion happened. The Indo-European language is the basis for all European languages except Basque.

If one considers the flow of population described, it seems clear to me that Basque (my great-maternal grandfather was a Basque) may be the survivor of the very early stream of homo sapiens that broke-off from Asia and entered Greece and then moved westward. But some say that the Basques were Aquitanians and are mentioned in Tacitus as fierce fighters against Rome. The GENOGRAPHICA project's maps may assist you in clearing up some of the movements noted.

The various language origins have been studied in various ways. One way is to trace languages is by their genetic origin and a recent study has the results depicted in the chart below that shows the approximate dates of the appearance of various languages.

To figure out how this may have come about, we first have to realize that humanoid types had, by the time that genetic changes created the first humans, peopled most of the contiguous lands of Africa and Asia. The advent of better-equipped human types apparently came about in that part of Africa named the Rift Valley. One must suppose that a good degree of intelligence had developed in the pre-humans and that the new type—homo sapiens sapiens—carried that intelligence to a higher level. These people, for whatever reasons, began to drift north and south. At that time they had some sort of communications beyond the grunts and trail denoted signs that were likely used by their precursors. I speculate that this first language was composed of a series of click sounds. Why? Because the only places on earth that such languages have been and are now heard is in only two places—the southwest of Africa and to the north of the Rift Valley; the language family is Khosian; the speakers are Bushmen and Hottentots. These are the routes that wandering primitive man may well have traveled on an initial journey out of the Rift Valley, with some members stopping off along the way and, over thousands of years, populating the areas behind the leading elements of the wanderers. Maps of languages in Africa clearly show that the click languages of the southwestern Bushmen and of the smaller enclave of click speakers to the north of the Rift Valley are isolated as if they, the leading elements, have reached their limit or, in the case of the northern group, had been constrained by other factors.

The following maps and classification are based on the work of the great linguist Joseph Greenberg, who died May 7, 2001 and were developed by Dr. Boeree, of Shippensberg University. Please understand that both the maps and statistics below are approximations but that the number of speakers applies to modern times

---

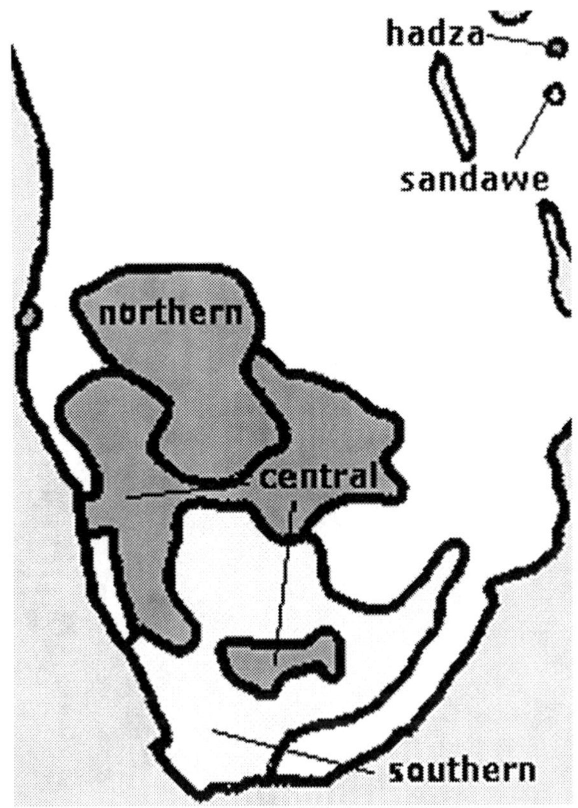

The Khoisan Family

About 30 languages with about 100,000 speakers, the Khoisan family includes the people we call the Bushmen and the Hottentots.

Some of the drifters who were not constrained in the north, went westerly and eventually, again over thousands of years, developed variants on the original languages. These have been identified as follows:

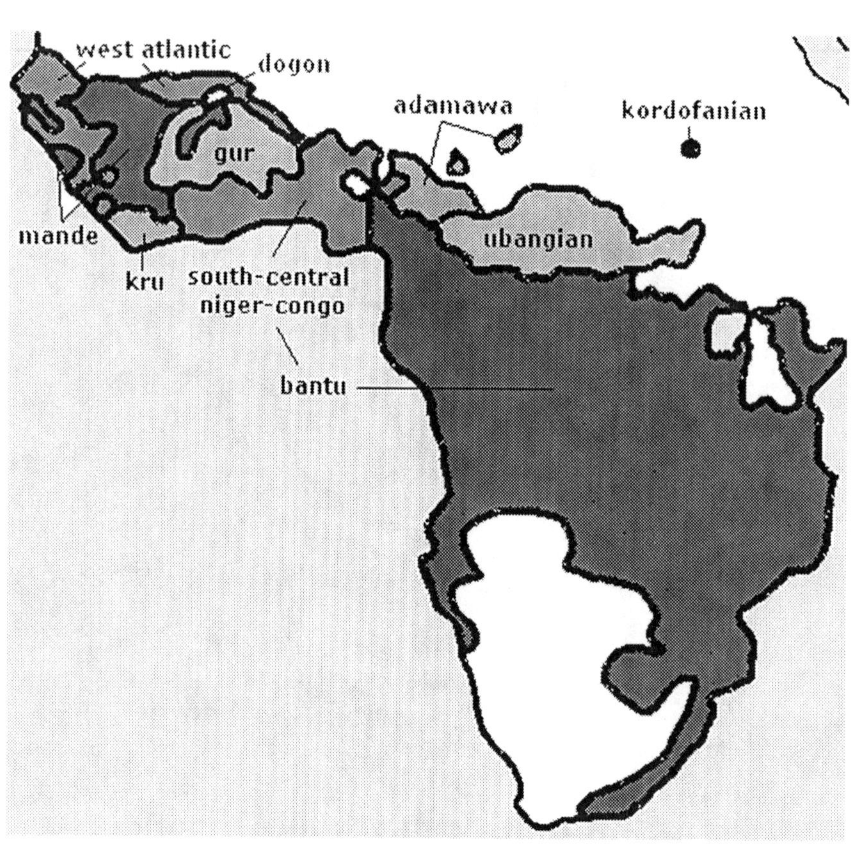

The Niger-Kordofanian Family

The largest sub-Saharan African family of languages, it includes some 1,000 languages with close to 200 million speakers. Best known are Mandinka, Swahili, Yoruba, and Zulu.

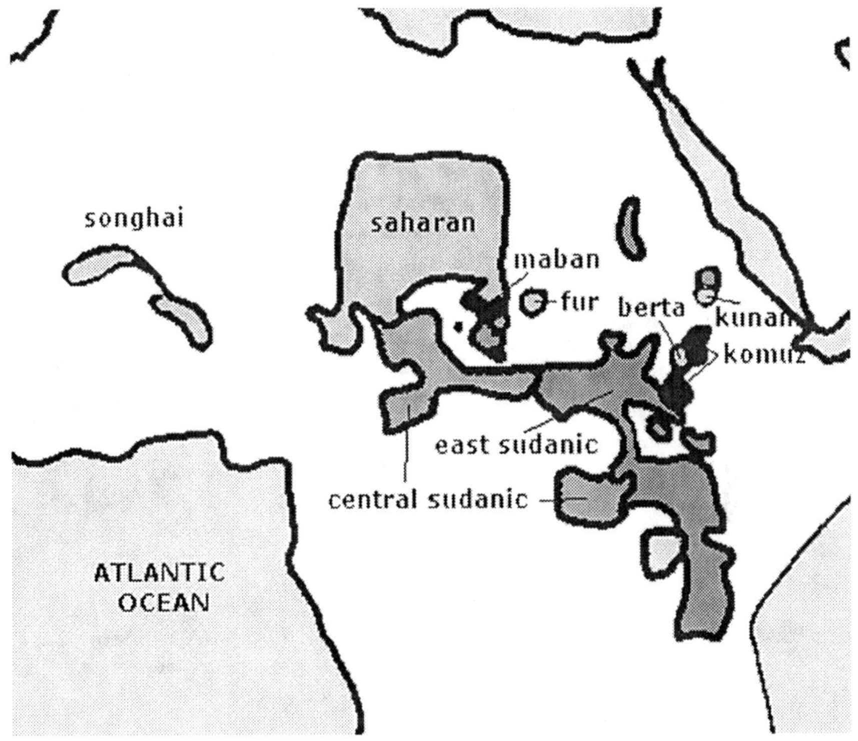

The Nilo-Saharan ("Hamitic") Family

With about 140 languages and 10 million speakers. The best known of these languages is Maasai, spoken by the tall warrior-herdsmen of east Africa.

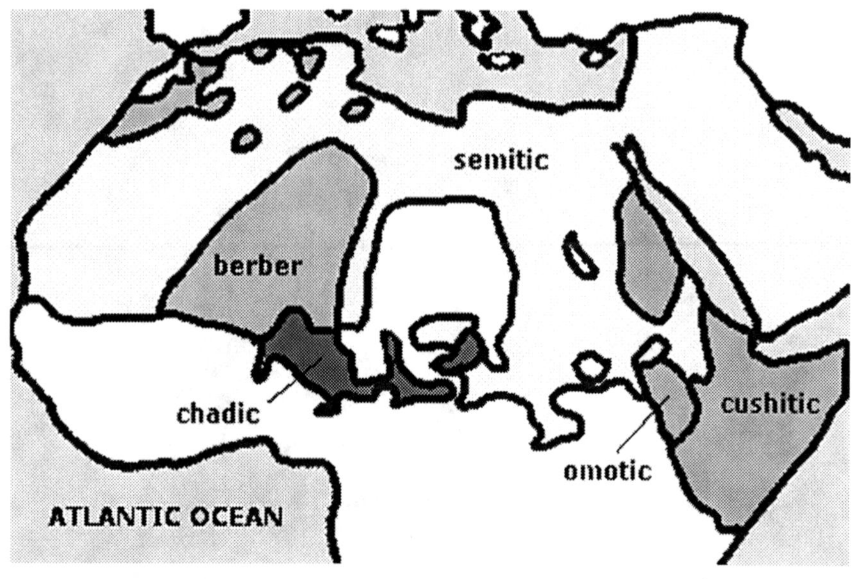

The Afro-Asiatic Family

This is a major language group, with 240 languages and 250 million speakers. It includes ancient Egyptian, Hebrew, and Aramaic, as well as the great Nigerian language Hausa. The many dialects of Arabic alone are spoken by as many as 200 million people.

The Indo-European Family
(with the isolates Basque, Burushaski, and Nahali)

The single largest language family, Indo-European has about 150 languages and about three billion speakers. Languages include Hindi and Urdu (400 million), Bengali (200 million), Spanish (300 million), Portuguese (200 million), French (100 million), German (100 million), Russian (300 million), and English (400 million) in Europe and the Americas. With English, one can reach approximately one billion people in the world.

There are three language isolates represented on this map, unrelated to any of the language families: Basque thrives between France and Spain. Burushaski and Nahali are found in the Indian subcontinent.

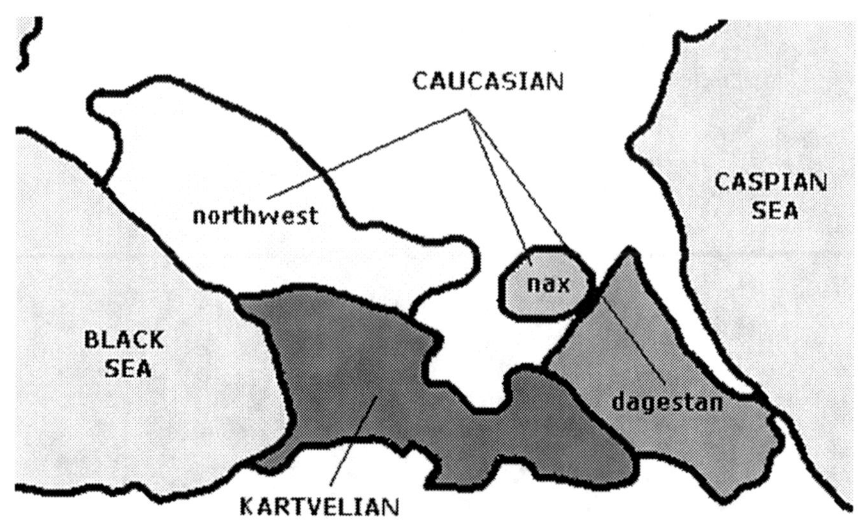

The Caucasian Family

There are 38 Caucasian languages between Russian and the Middle East, with about five million speakers. Abkhasian and Chechenian are the most familiar.

The Kartvelian languages are considered by many linguists to be a separate family, possibly related to Indo-European. Its prime example is Georgian.

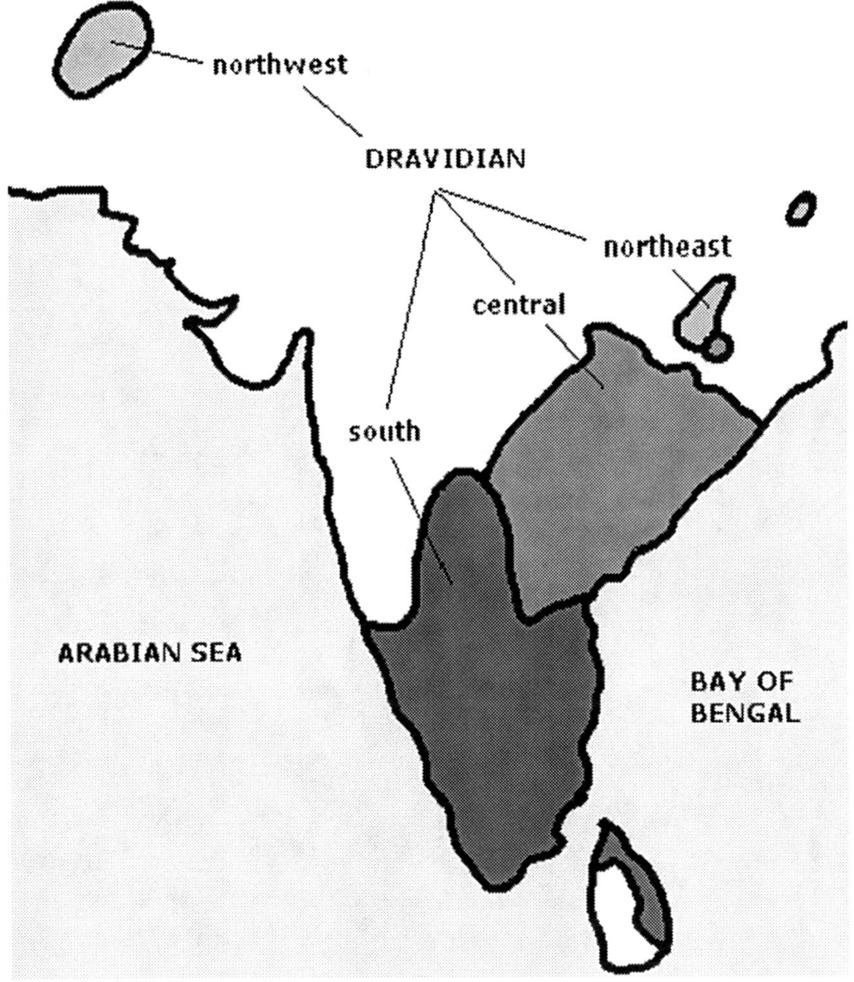

The Dravidian Family

These are the "old" languages of India, with about 25 representataties and 150 million speakers. Best known are Tamil and Telugu.

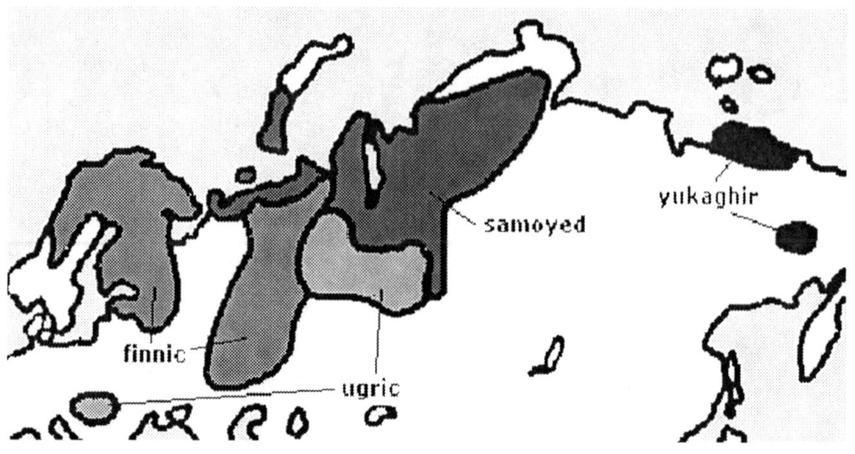

The Uralic-Yukaghir Family

There are about 20 languages with 20 million speakers in this family. Best known are Finnish, Estonian, Hungarian, and Saami, the language of the Lapplanders.

The Altaic Family
(with the isolates Ket and Gilyak)

There are about 60 langauges in the Altaic family, with about 250 million speakers. Included are Turkish and Mongolian.

There is considerable controversy about this family. First, it is often classified with the Uralic languages (see above), which have a similar grammatic structures.

Second, many linguists doubt that Korean, Japanese (125 million speakers), or Ainu should be included, or that these last three are even related to each other!

Also represented here are the language isolates Gilyak and Ket.

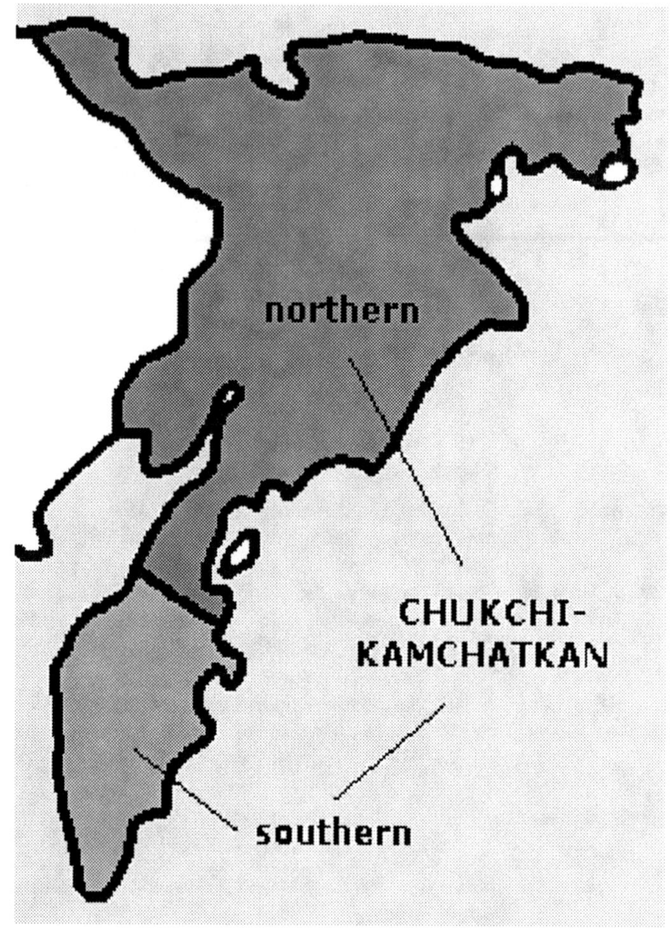

The Chukchi-Kamchatkan ("Paleosiberian") Family

Perhaps the smallest family, this one includes 5 languages with 23,000 speakers in the farthest northeastern reaches of Siberia. Many linguists consider these two unrelated families.

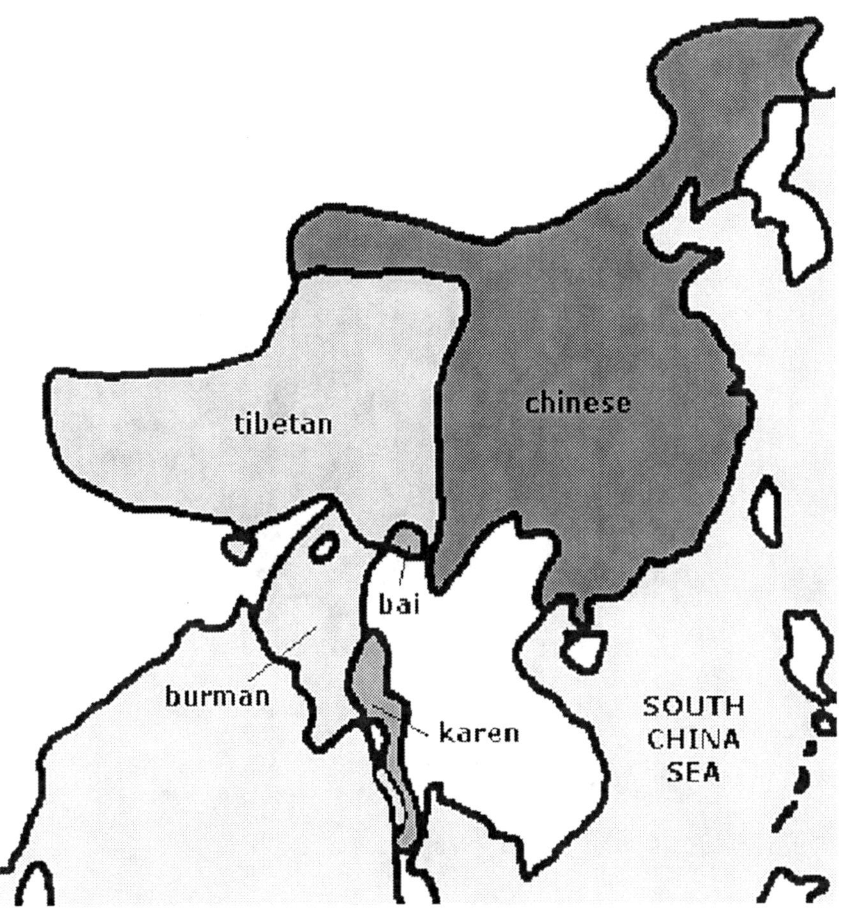

The Sino-Tibetan Family

A very important language family, it includes some 250 languages. Mandarin Chinese (Putonghua) alone is spoken by one billion people!

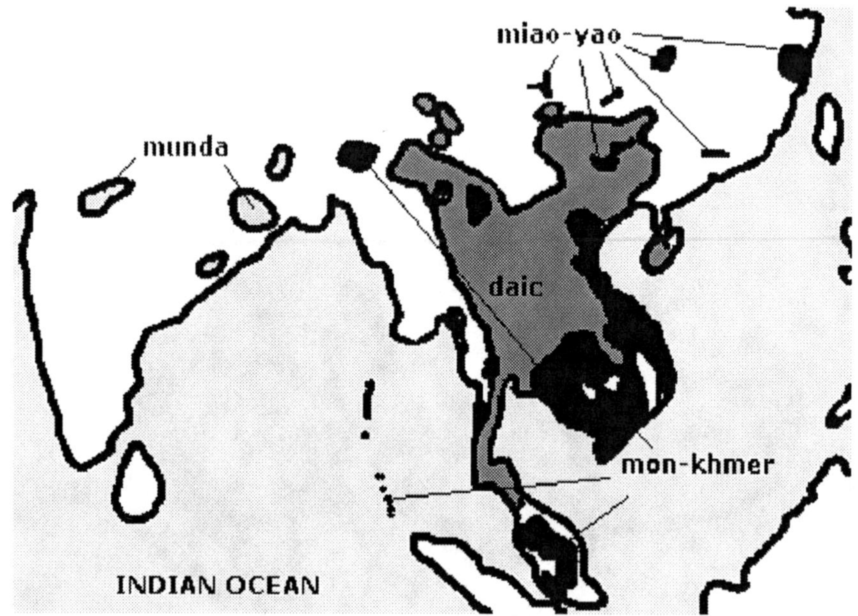

The Miao-Yao, Austro-Asiatic, and Daic Families

Austro-Asiatic (Munda in India and Mon-Khmer in southeast Asia) has 150 languages and 60 million speakers, including Vietnamese.

Miao-Yao consists of four langauges with seven million speakers, scattered all over southern China and southeast Asia generally.

Daic has some 60 languages with 50 million speakers, especially Thai (Siamese).

These three language families are sometimes grouped with the Austronesian family (below) into a "superfamily" called Austric. On the other hand, some linguists consider Miao-Yao and Daic relatives of Chinese.

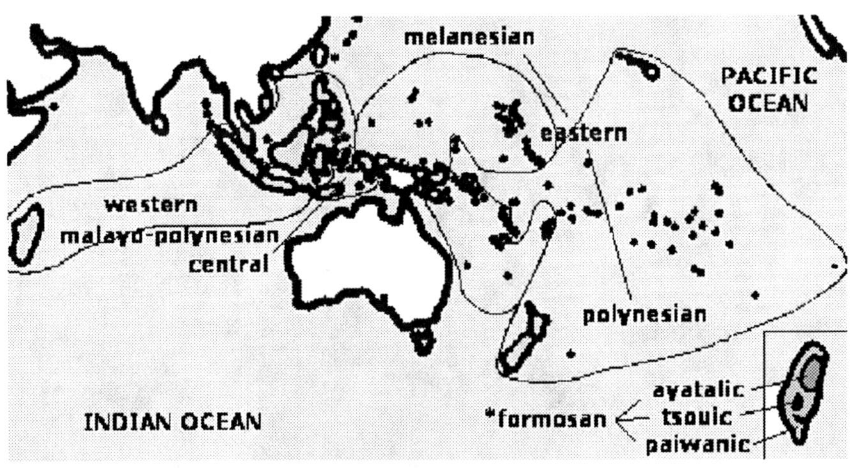

The Austronesian Family

This family includes some 1000 different languages, spoken by about 250 million speakers. Malay and Indonesian (essentially the same language) account for about 140 million. Other examples include Malagasy in Africa, Tagalog in the Philippines, the aboriginal languages of Formosa (Taiwan)—now almost displaced by Chinese—and the many languages of the Pacific Islands, from Hawaiian in the north Pacific to Maori in New Zealand.

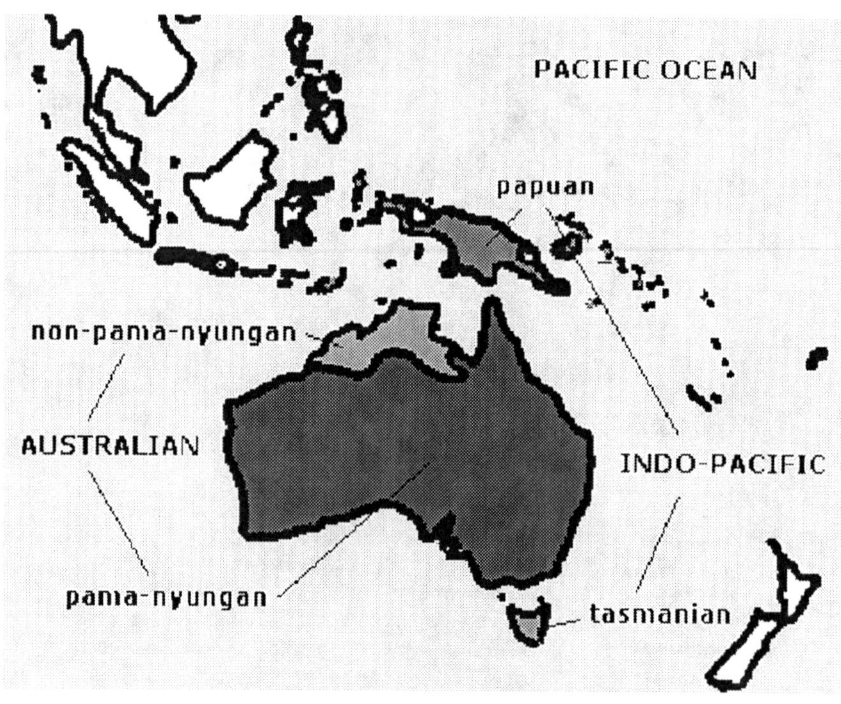

The Indo-Pacific and Australian Families

There are about 700 languages in the Indo-Pacific family, most of them in the island of New Guinea, with about 3 million speakers. Many linguists are not at all convinced that all these languages are related. In fact, a number of them have yet to be studied! On the other hand, some believe that the family may include Tasmanian, now extinct.

Possibly related are the 170 languages of the Australian aborigines. Sadly, there are only about 30,000 native speakers left.

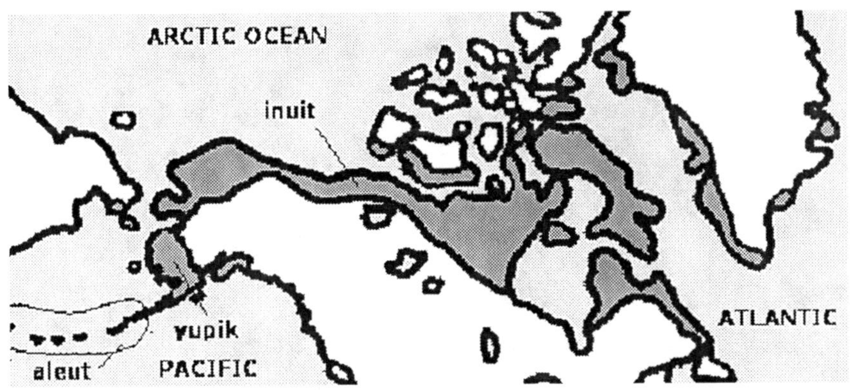

The Eskimo-Aleut Family

The Eskimo-Aleut family consists of nine languages, spoken by about 85,000 people. The Inuit now effectively control Greenland (Kalaallit Nunaat) and the Canadian territory of Nunavat.

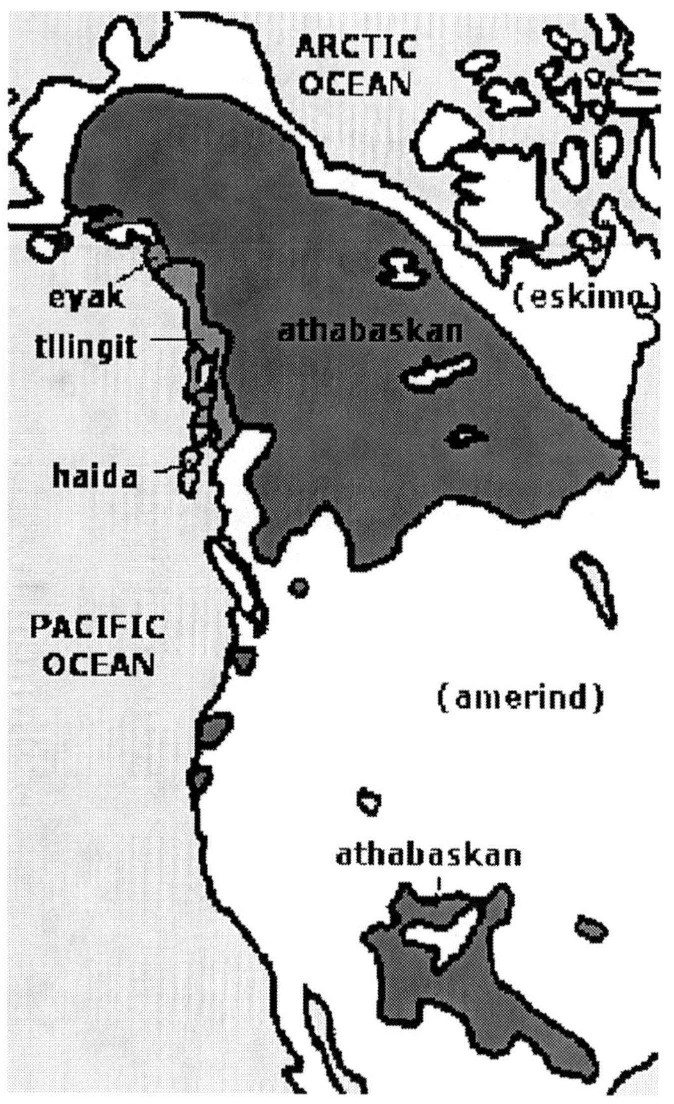

The Na-Dene Family

This family includes 34 languages spoken by about 200,000 people. Best known examples are Tlingit, Haida, Navaho, and Apache.

The Amerind Family (North America)

Although many linguists do not accept the idea that all North and South American Indian languages (other than the Na-Dene and Eskimo-Aleut) can be classified into one family, it is often accepted for convenience sake. Amerind includes nearly 600 languages, with more than 20 million speakers. In North America, some of the best known names are Ojibwa and Cree, Dakota (or Sioux), Cherokee and Iroquois, Hopi and Nahuatl (or Aztec), and the Mayan languages.

The Amerind Family (South America)

The language map of South America includes some of the North American sub-families, and adds a few more. Well known languages include Quechua (Inca), Guarani, and Carib. The Andean language sub-family (which includes Quechua) numbers nearly nine million speakers!

Posted on July 15, 2000; revisions posted Nov. 25, 2003

APPENDIX D

THE HERO IN MYTH AND LITERTURE

The Hero in Myth and Literature

The following pages are the lecture notes I used during my presentations of a course in mythology during the 1980s and 1990s. This excerpt deals with the material that made Joseph Campbell famous in the field, the hero's journey, about which Campbell studied some 1,000 versions of the journey in many languages. The lecture begins as follows:

The hero journey is really an inward psychological drama. Each of us is a hero in some aspect during our lives and what makes a hero has been the subject of innumerable discussions and writings.

Each hero has his 'road of trials' as one pushes on through life to gain our individuality, sense of integrated personality, sense of purpose and our sense of place. While we will look at the hero in a classical sense, remember that each of us is a hero—from breaking away from one's mother's hand to get to the first First Grade class—alone among strangers—to departing a familiar nest and going away to college or to the Marine boot camp, to graduating … and so on. Always there is a striving and a set of trials and, if successful, a gain to oneself or to others.

The call to adventure lifts us out of everyday lives where we focus on everyday matters and individual problems to an engagement with larger problems. When Luke Skywalker sees the hologram of Princess Leia and learns her story, he learns that he is not the only one in trouble, society is in trouble and there are problems larger and more important than his own. In 'The Wizard of OZ', Dorothy has a problem—she is an orphan and does not have a sense of place or a goal in the troubled world of the farm—the society is in danger, it is in a depression. When

Dorothy sets a goal, overcomes the Wicked Witch, she is on the road to a confrontation between good and evil. This theme is inherent and basic in many hero myths and can be seen in the currently again popular works of J.R.R. Tolkien where an ordinary person—Frodo—is chosen to perform an important task for the benefit of his society.

The hero in myth has been examined, never more thoroughly than by Joseph Campbell in "The Hero With a Thousand Faces". He considered thousands of hero stories from all over the world and identified the typical hero journey about as shown in the drawing now distributed. Let me read you what Campbell has written about this journey. Please follow on the drawing from the top and to the left:

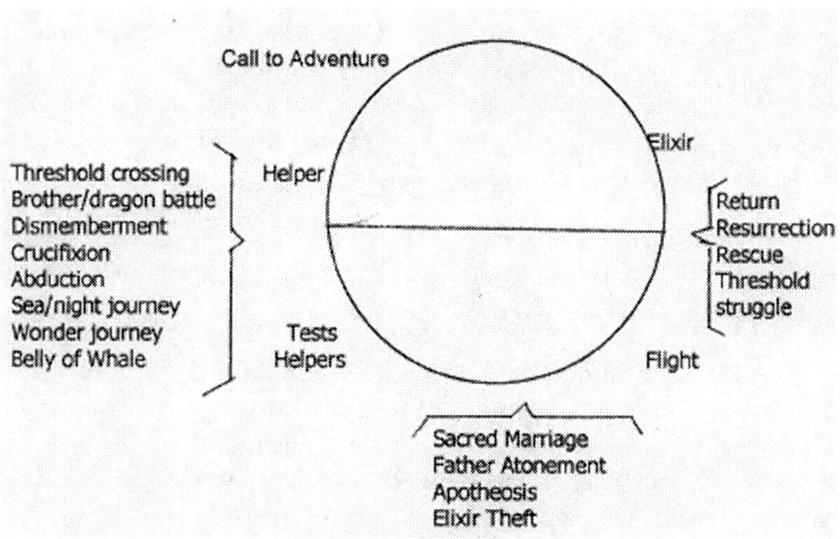

The mythological hero, setting forth from his common day hut or castle, is lured, carried away, or voluntarily proceeds, to the threshold of adventure. There he encounters a shadow presence or thing that guards his passage. The hero may overcome, defeat or conciliate this power and go alive into the [unconscious] kingdom of the dark [brother battle, dragon battle, offering, charm] or be slain by the opponent and descend in death, or dismemberment or crucifixion. Beyond the threshold, then, the hero journeys through a world of unfamiliar yet strangely intimate forces, some of which severely threaten him by tests, some of which give magical aid via helpers. When he arrives at the nadir of his mythological round, he undergoes supreme ordeal and gains his reward. This triumph may be represented by the hero's sexual union with the goddess-mother of the world, as in a sacred marriage, or his recognition by the father-creator in an atonement, by his own divination or apotheosis, or—if the powers have remained unfriendly to him—by the theft of the boon he came to gain represented by a bride-theft or a fire-theft or such. Intrinsically this is an expansion of consciousness and of being as in a transfiguration, illumination, or freedom. The final work is that of return. If the powers have blessed the hero, he now sets forth with a protective emissary; if not, he flees and is pursued [a transformation flight or an obstacle flight]. At the return threshold the transcendental powers must remain behind; the hero emerges from the unconscious kingdom of the dead in a return and resurrection. The boon he brings with him restores him and or the world."

All these stages are summarized in the drawing handed out, which is from Campbell's book.

Not all of these happenings concern each hero, as heroes come in all shapes and sizes. However many important heroes have singular beginnings, as we shall see. As hero myths are metaphors for our search for self-knowledge they speak to our efforts for individuation. **To follow the hero is to find ourselves**. The passage of the mythological hero may be over the ground, incidentally; fundamentally it is inward—into depths where obscure resistances are overcome, and forgotten powers are revivified and made available for the transfiguration of the locality of the hero **or of the world. As one can see, the** journey involves separation, initiation, and return.

These stages can be seen in the traditional legend of The Great Struggle of the Buddha.

He went from his palace one day and, on successive days, saw an old decrepit man, a diseased man, a dead man, and a monk. He learned that the monk had retired from the world. A few days later, he left his palace, cut his hair and assumed the garments of a monk, living as a beggar until he had acquired and transcended the eight stages of meditation. **He had answered a call to his destiny**. He had practiced the **Noble Eightfold Path** that is constituted by right (correct) **views**, right **aspirations, right speech, right conduct or vocation, right livelihood, right effort, right mindfulness, and right meditation attainment or rapture.**

One day he sat in contemplation beneath a tree and received a signal through a bowl floating upstream after he had discarded it that his destiny was at hand. He rose and proceeded along a road garlanded with flowers to **the Bo Tree—the tree of enlightenment (compare with the Bible story of Eden) under which he was to redeem the universe.** The dangerous gods then appeared and tried to interfere with the Buddha by, first, threatening him with an army but he was unmoved; second, by tempting him with Desire, Pining, and Lust—in the form of maidens—but he was not distracted; and, finally, by the dangerous gods attempting to kill him, but he merely touched the Earth, whereupon the Earth scattered the challenging hosts.

Having won this initial victory, the Buddha acquired, first, knowledge of his previous existences; then he acquired the divine eye of omniscient vision, and understanding of the chain of causation. **At the break of day he experienced perfect enlightenment. This is the single most important moment in Oriental mythology, akin to the crucifixion of Jesus for Christians.** After this the Buddha began to proclaim the path, **the way, to enlightenment, not enlightenment itself but the means to achieve it.** This doctrine about the incommunicability of the truth about enlightenment is basic to Oriental traditions.

His Birth and Situation

The hero must be a unique person but one with whom we can identify, usually shedding mortal ties. Thus **Thesus,** Hero of the Minotaur legend, was born of a God who chose a mortal woman for the hero's mother and the hero's way into the world. So he is mortal but possessed of certain human attributes.

Those heroes who are also born of mortal woman chosen by a god include Jesus, son of God and Mother Mary; Hercules, son of Zeus and mother Alcemene; and Helen of Troy, daughter of Zeus and Leda or Nemesis.

The same can be said for Krishna, an incarnation of Vishnu, whom we met in the creation myth, and who is the preserver God into whose being the worlds are absorbed and born again. Variously he was conceived by a ghost, or was conceived by a virgin. There was renewal of his mother's virginity and his abandonment beside a river. He was adopted by lower classes, and given a divine sign. There are similarities here with **the tale of Moses (about 8th XC BCE)**, who was left in a basket by a river and adopted; with **Siegfried**, incestuous son of brother and sister, who was left in a glass in a river and adopted by a doe and a blacksmith; and the tale **of Perseus**, born of a princess Danae, who, being imprisoned, was conceived by Zeus in a shower of gold. The mother and child were then cast into the sea in a box, which a fisherman drew ashore. Compare these themes with that of **Oedipus** who was abandoned and left to die but was raised by a shepherd.

And mortals, too, captured these themes as when **Sargon** (2,350 BCE) proclaimed (in a recorded fragment) "Sargon am I, the mighty king, Monarch of Agade. My lowly mother conceived and bore me in secrecy; placed me in a basket of rushes; sealed it with bitumen, and set me in a river ... The river bore me up and carried me to Akku, the irrigator, who took me from the river, raised me as his son, and made of me a gardener. While I was a gardener, the Goddess Ishtar loved me. Then I ruled the Kingdom."

In these tales there is the idea that an important person—a world child and the hope of a new beginning—must be born or touched by the eternal waters that represent the eternal Mother Goddess. The hero cannot belong to any single mortal family—he belongs to all humanity. Reflect, are we not all born of water? And is not baptism a central rite of most churches?

Note the **following themes**—

Miraculous Conception—this gives the hero a special status. Both Jesus and the Aztec God, Quetzalcoatl, were born of virgins. Buddha conceives himself in his mother's dream; Adonis is conceived and born of a tree; Mithras was born of a rock, in a cave and attended by shepherds on a date that we now know was December 25th.

Search for a Father—The hero is often abandoned so that he will become a person not related to a specific family, but related to the world. He searches for the real source of his genesis, which may transcend the biological Father. Thus the command "Find your Father" often appears in hero stories.

Hero Birth—often born in a dark place—a cave, a grove, a stable, a water-pot as symbolic of the womb that prefigures the tomb.

The Journey Quest of the Hero and the Call to Adventure

The Quest and Call to Adventure

Typical of the circumstances of a call often are; a dark forest, a great tree, a babbling brook; and the appearance of an ugly carrier of the power of destiny (a dragon, a frog, a snake, etc). The call to adventure or trial can be seen, for example, as the voice of **God from a burning bush**, the **appearance of the Grail** to Arthur's knights of the Round Table, the **call to the Buddha of the four signs** (floating bowl, attacks defeated, women spurned, and challenge), and the voice to Mohammed that said "Write".

The quest is marked by trials, confrontations, defeats of monsters representing inner fears, and traumas. In patriarchal societies there are temptresses—Circe, Sirens, Delilah, and the Femme Fatale. Sometimes the hero dallies but the true hero is not diverted (look what happened to a diverted Sampson).

Here are some other examples of the call:

<u>Joan d'Arc</u>—voices call her to her task, trial, and death

<u>Oedipus</u>—the call to remove the moral pollution destroying Thebes, and the quest for identity of self and Father. His quest confirms his worst fears—he kills his Father and marries his own Mother.

<u>King Arthur</u>—the call to adventure is a sword, stabbed into a rock that can only be removed by a pure king. The quest is for renewal via a search for the Holy Grail. He and his knights must face the Femme Fatale—Morgan le Fay (mistress of Merlin), Vivian, and the Lady of the Lake—and deal with Guinevere. Here let me call your attention to a book, "The Witch of the North", by Courtney Jones and his "In The Shadow of the Oak King".

<u>Thesus</u>—the call is via a sword and sandals hidden at his birth under a magic rock. After getting these he travels to Athens clearing the way of robbers, hears the horrid tale of an annual tribute of 14 young people for a monster in Crete, goes there, confronts and slays it (the Minotaur) with the aid of a helper (Ariadne), returning to Athens, having neglected to inform his Father of his return, causes that man to commit suicide.

<u>Refusal of the Call</u>

Sometimes those called make an initial refusal to respond. Proverbs I.24–27. 32 says "Because I have called, and ye refused.... I also will laugh at your calamity; I will mock when your fear cometh; when your fear cometh as desolation, and your destruction cometh as a whirlwind; when distress and anguish come over you." "For the turning away of the simple shall slay them, and the prosperity of fools shall destroy them".

The refusal is essentially a refusal to give up one's own interests

For example:

Moses—called by an angel from a burning bush, refuses and then accepts

Jesus—in the garden

Parcival—a quest for the Grail and a failure—akin to refusal of a call

Jonah—refuses the order to go to Nineveh and was swallowed by a whale; he later accepts the call.

Crossing the Threshold

With an idea of a destiny to aid him, the hero goes forward until he comes to the threshold guardian (s). **Beyond them is darkness and a lack of protection from his compatriots or tribe**—thus the sailors of Columbus; explorers in the entire world; and other heroes such as rescuers and our children as they venture from the security and assurance of the family into the uncertainties and challenges of—college.

The god Pan is a well-known classical example of a threshold guardian, dwelling just beyond the protected zone of the village boundary. He was the inventor of the pipes and his music inspired panic in those who accidentally ventured into his domain. But, to those who paid him worship, he was benign, granting bounty to all and entrance to his orgiastic rites.

The threshold is often guarded by two imagoes or ogres, symbolizing the pairs of opposites in nature (being, not being; life and death; good and evil; etc) {remember this theme?]. Among these guardians are the clashing rocks at sea through which the hero always passes—the rocky islands of the Euxine Sea that clashed together to kill travelers, and through which Jason sailed, are legend. The twin heroes of the Navaho legend of the Spider Woman, who warned the two who were seeking their father of the four places of danger—rocks that crush, reeds that cut; cactuses that tear; and boiling sands—made it safely through their trials with the aid of this knowledge and the eagle feathers she gave them.

Transit through this area of enchantment may also involve being swallowed by a whale (Jonah) and appearing to have died as in the legend of Hiawatha:

Mishe-Naha, King of Fishes,
In his wrath he darted upward,
Flashing leaped into the sunshine,
Opened his great jaws and swallowed
Both canoe and Hiawatha.

Little Red Ridinghood was swallowed by a wolf, and the entire Greek Pantheon (except for Zeus) was swallowed by Kronos!.

The disappearance corresponds in a sense to the passing of a worshiper into a temple. The temple interior, the belly of the whale, and the heavenly land above, beyond, and below the confines of the world are one and the same. That is why gargoyles, dragons, and other images guard temple approaches. Once inside the votary may be said to have died to time and returned to the World Navel, earthly Paradise. Allegorically then, the passage into the temple and the hero dive into the jaws of the whale are identical adventures, both denoting a life-centering and life-renewing act.

A Guide or Helper

Mythology supplies instances of guides such as a wizard, an old man, a hermit, a shepherd or, again, a ferryman to conduct souls to the afterworld. Classically this guide is Hermes-Mercury and, in Christian settings, the Holy Ghost and the Virgin. In Egyptian tales it is Thoth (a god of the moon, of reckoning, of learning, and of writing). Other examples are:

Aeneas is guided by the Sybil through the underworld in his search for his Father. After getting the Golden Bough to enter, and after traversing the Elysian Fields (where the dead were buried) Aeneas returned to the world of the living.

Obe Ben Kenobe—the wise old man of the 'Star Wars' movie, in the making of which Joseph Campbell was the mythological adviser, guides and advises Luke. Go see this as a hero journey and identify the many allusions to matters we deal with here.

In like vein the guide may be a fairy godmother or a kindly witch—of the West?

Ariadne, whose gift of thread enabled Theseus to escape the labyrinth of Minos in Crete,

Spider Woman, whom we have met just above in the role of helper.

Gandolf, the wise man of the Tolkien stories

Threats to the Hero's Life

Just **as one part of a society or individual wishes for stability, so another part desires change.** In myth there are forces that may literally set the hero adrift (in a basket on a river, or leave him alone in the wilderness) or which threaten him (via dragons, demons, angry or jealous fathers, etc). All these forces are willing to hinder the hero in his travel and quest. In psychological terms, there is a part of us that clings to safety and the nest, and this part resists the journey of self-discovery. The hero must separate himself or be separated from human frailties in order to continue the journey of self-discovery.

Death is faced often in hero stories. A journey to the land of the dead (see Aeneas, above) represents a journey to the depths of one's unconscious world where individual or human destinies lie. **In facing death we rob it of its dominion over us and emerge from the underworld to be reborn—as from a second womb, as represented by the psychryast's couch—into a new, whole individual existence.**

The return from the underworld is often accompanied by the bringing of **a great new good—a new crop (as in the tale of Hiawatha) or new knowledge for the general use of mankind or for the use of the hero. The allusion here is to Jesus, who brings hope and salvation to mankind.**

In this context of hope and salvation, I want to relate to you what Edward Gibbon says in 'The Decline and Fall of the Roman Empire' about why Christianity spread and took hold in its early days. Recall that those days were ones of daily terror from unexpected illness; from the opprobrium of a variety of pagan Gods, none of whom one could be certain about; from the depredations of neighbors or invader; and from a host of inexplicable matters. Many pagan religions held their followers in thrall to a variety of fearful rites. There were only terrors at the end of life and either a relegation to torments or to some other sort of unexplained situation.

Gibbon states that there were five reasons for the spread and acceptance of Christianity of which, I think, the most important was the hope of a salvation and a better prospect at the end of life than might be achieved during it. **In a world of**

no hope, Christianity brought hope. He gives these five reasons as—1. the zeal of the Christians and their softer approach than that of the Jews to attracting new adherents; 2. the doctrine of a future and pleasant life; 3. miraculous powers ascribed to the early church; 4. the pure and austere morals of the Christians; and 5. the union and discipline among Christians and the manner in which their organization formed an increasing and independent 'state' within the Roman Empire, until Christianity became the dominant religion and practice in the Roman world.

While the writing of Gibbon is now viewed as old fashioned, with long clausal sentences, it is to be viewed with amazement for the sheer scholarship that produced the epic. My Penguin paperback of 789 pages and contains only excerpts from Gibbon's original 51 Chapters. If you read some of it you will learn more than you need to about Rome.

This theme of death and resurrection is from eons ago and is part of the Great Mother myth as seen in the dying and resurrected gods of the ancient planting cultures, and the practices of killing the king and scattering his pieces to fructify the fields and bring new crops. Read Chapter 24 of Frazer's 'The Golden Bough" for more detail of practices that lasted to the 19th XC.

Further to the ideas herein, read again Wm. Faulkner's "The Bear"—Ike's quest through life for its meaning. Perhaps the most famous hero quest is to be found in "Ulysses", retold in modern times by James Joyce's "Finnegans Wake". There is an interesting key to the myths of "the Wake" by Joseph Campbell called "A Skeleton Key to Finnegans Wake"; although difficult to find, it is available at Amazon. Also recall both **Hamlet** and **King Lear** who must die so that their societies may become normal again, and so that the audience may realize a new path toward individual understanding.

Overcoming Challenges

An essential part of the journey **involves trials and challenges.**

Heracles, illegitimate son of Zeus by Alcemene, was abandoned, killed his wife and children, freed Prometheus (who had stolen fire from Zeus and was punished by being chained to a rock where an eagle pecked at his liver daily) was made immortal by a Goddess, and suffered many trials (the 12 labors) and threats.

Others in this mode are—**Zoroaster** (about whom a note is appended below), **Jesus, Siegfried who were threatened by demons, Satan, and a dragon respectively.**

In India, Buddha follows the hero path—miraculously conceived and born without impurity; possessed of adult and more abilities as a boy, his mother dies early in his life—so that he represents the eternal child, pure and unsullied and not tied to any human being, who comes to clear the world of sin and folly.

Note about Zoroaster

I am pausing here to acquaint you with a very old religion that is still practiced by many Indians around Bombay and in a few other places in India. They are called Parses (parsee or Persians) and practice Zoroasterism as a religion. Zoroaster was a man born about 630–620 BCE in what is now Iran, near Tehran. This dating would place him before Alexander the Great and the time of Ezekiel a major Hebrew prophet. Zoroaster had revelations through a supreme god—and in this we must recognize that he was an **early monotheistic leader**—called Ahura Mazda, father of the Holy Spirit and of justice, truth and righteous thought. He stated that god and man must obey the same principles. Zoroaster converted a king and his religion became the accepted one, displacing the previous polytheism. It spread throughout the Middle East and reached India. On another level, the god of Zoaraster lives on in our memory through the word Mazda, meaning light as in Mazda Lamps, because the religion revered the flames of the unquenchable gas/oil eruptions that, even today, are alight in Iran (Persia).

As another note, *can you credit that Zoroaster, Lao-Tzu, Buddha, Mahavira (founder of the Jain religion of austerity) and Pythagoras were all citizens of the 600BCE era.*

The Search

Buddha searches for enlightenment under the Bodi Tree that represents *axis mundi*, the world center tree (again) of life [the tree, it is said, still exists in India]. **Aeneas** searches for Rome, the new Troy; and **Ulysses** searches for a way to return home. **Rama** searches for his wife, a story often told and retold. A contemporary tracing of Rama's search is to be found in "The Arrow of the Blue Skinned God", by Jonah Blank. **Tristan** searches for Isolde and **Jason's search is well known** since 3rd XC BCE in tellings by Pindar and Euripedes.

Temptations and Tests

Once across the threshold of adventure, the Hero is in a dream-=time landscape of fluid and ambiguous forms and faces temptations as well as trials as he is urged on to his destiny. The Indian story of Buddha and his temptations (by threat, bribe, and lust) is similar to that of Jesus and his temptations. **Note, too, that the Bodi Tree has an analogue in the Tree of Knowledge of Good and Evil in Eden of the Old Testament, and in the Cross of Calvary, which is also the tree of Knowledge of Everlasting life and a tenuous association with the Bodi tree's enlightenment.**

Then, too, Hiawatha who, after a journey of fasting and self-denial strives to bring back a boon to mankind. I have already mentioned Hercules/Heracles and his trails and tests. There is **also Perseus** (killed the Medusa), **Oedipus** who destroyed the Sphinx after answering his riddle (does anyone know what was the riddle?). **Saint George** who slew the dragon in order to free the maiden, **Theseus** who slew the **Minotaur** and returned safely from the Labarynth.

Look, too, at the tale of Sir Gawain and the Green Knight, recently re-told in a contemporary setting by Iris Murdoch in "The Green Knight". This deals with revenge, remorse, betrayal, and forgiveness as the characters play out their roles. The original tale, translated from the original Anglo-Saxon by Tolkien while a Professor at Oxford, is also worth re-reading.

These trials and tests often need explanation or support from a helper, as the way is dangerous. Here the shaman comes in all guises from priest, to politician, to doctor, to leader, and to common man such as thee man who led the 9/11 charge in the airplane over Pennsylvania. It is the guide who can lead the hero, the nation, or the tribe toward self-understanding or to dealing with the fears to be faced.

Rebirth and Apotheosis (achievement of godhood)

The *motif of rebirth or resurrection is common in myth*. It is actually or by implication found in, for example, the practices of Attis, Osiris, Jonah, the Blackfoot tribe myth of Kutoyis, and the tale of Heracles and Quetzalcoatl and in the story of Jesus and Mary, Queen of Heaven.

I will leave it to you to look at Attis, Dionysus and Osiris, but *meeting the Godhead or the Goddess is symbolized in the notion of 'The Lady of the House of Sleep'.*

We meet her in many tales as a variant **of Brunhilde and Briar-Rose** (forever entombed in protection that requires immense effort to approach). She is the paragon of beauty, the ultimate desire, the goal of the hero quest. In a sense she is mother, sister, mistress, and bride but unattainable except through extra effort. She is the maiden rescued by an unselfish St. George from an imprisonment that denies her true purpose. The dragon cannot treat her or use her as a maiden and while the dragon guards her, the rest of her world cannot function properly. More than the maiden is set free by the hero.

In overcoming the protections, be they protection of thorns or dragons, we come to realize the meaning of true love for all and for ourselves and to recognize our frailties. **But sometimes the Goddess is not benign.** Recall the approvals of killing that the chaste and terrible Diana (not the Princess) inflicted upon Acteon, who had viewed her naked.

Finally, realizing enlightenment, as did Buddha, is also to be seen as an apotheosis and transfiguration to a new, higher level of comprehension of the world and its purpose and of its inhabitants.

Atonement with the Father

Mythologically the "at-one-ment" with the Father consists of becoming whole as a personality through the abandonment of self-generated double monsters. One of these is the "superego", to use Freud's term, or the dragon thought to be God that provides moral standards but is often weakened. The other is the repressed "id" or the dragon thought to be sin and the site of more primitive instincts. The terrible God of the Hebrews, sending plagues, tempests and retributions, and the terrible God of the Puritans, with fire and brimstone withheld from the sinner only by God's pleasure, known as mercy and grace, is seen to be the fate of man. Only by atonement can a better fate be assumed.

In other mythologies, terror is better balanced. "Fear not", says the hand gesture of Shiva while he dances the destruction of the present universe, for there will be others. The magic of the sacraments, the power of primitive amulets (many Greeks and North American Indians carry an eye of glass to ward off evil spirits or keep garlic over their doors), and **the supernatural helpers of myth are mankind's assurance that the arrow, the flames, and the flood may not be as brutal and incomprehensible as they may seem.**

Resurrection

Most know of Jesus but few know **of Osiris, Dionysus and Attis**, all torn apart and resurrected. This theme symbolizes the return to the world we know of a new God bearing a boon for mankind, Be it grain or corn, or salvation and eternal life, our deeper understanding of the universe is made more true and complete by the resurrection.

The Return

Having won the blessing of God or Goddess, the hero is sent back to the world with some boon—deeper understanding, a vision to pass on, or a gift for mankind—for the restoration of society or himself. The return may be a flight if the hero has not pleased the Gods or if he has been forced to steal the boon or gift. It can be complicated by magical obstructions (Perseus fleeing with the head of Medusa or Jason's difficult involvement with Medea) to his passing out of the dream-world, *for passing out of the dream world is difficult if we have forgotten that the divine and the human are aspects of one dimension of reality.*

Summary

This whole journey can be illustrated, remembering as we read, by the **Tale of Peter Rabbit.** You will realize why this tale is a perennial favorite of all children, perhaps more open to the implications than are we adults.

Peter gets a call in a negative way—**"Don't go into Mr. McGregor's garden**"—but he goes and leaves the known safe world of his mother and siblings. There is a threshold crossing as he squeezes under the gate and enters another world. Peter faces many tests and terrors in a shed, where he goes into the belly of the whale in the form of a jar and, caught in a net is freed by the urging of helper birds. Peter flees from the hacking of Mr. McGregor trying to find a way out, finds one gate closed and finally gets to the entrance again and squeezes out. He has done what his Father did not do—escape. But it is not the same Peter. He has left something of himself behind in the garden. He has shed his shoes and blue coat that is the symbol of his perseverance and escape. Peter returns with his knowledge of a wider world and of himself—a new Peter.

And the almost universal meaning of the hero journey has been co-opted by legend makers who wished to make their particular heroes seem more relevant. We can see this in the following legends:

King Sargon of Agade (2550BCE) was born of a lowly mother. His father was unknown. Set adrift in a basket of bulrushes on the waters of the Euphrates, he was discovered by Akki the husbandsman and brought up to be a gardner. The goddess Ishtar favoured the youth so that he became, at last, King and Emperor.

Chandragupta (4th XC BCE) founder of the Hindu Maurya dynasty, was abandoned in an earthen jar at the threshold of a cowshed. A herdsman discovered and fostered the infant. One day while playing a game Chandragupta performed a miracle and, being observed in this by a passing noble, was taken into another home where it was discovered that he was a Maurya.

Pope Gregory the Great (540–604 CE) was born of noble twins who, at the devil's urging, committed incest. Gregory was set to sea in a casket by his mother. He was found and raised by fishermen and at age 6 was sent to be educated as a priest. He wished, however, to be a warrior and, departing came to the land of his parents where he won the hand of the Queen—his mother. Gregory, on discovering this additional incest, spent the next 7 years in penance, chained to a rock in the sea. The keys to the chain were tossed into the sea but when a fish was caught with the keys in its belly, it was taken as a providential sign. The penitent was taken to Rome where, in due course, he became Pope. (This legend is from 'The Myth of the Birth of the Hero' by Otto Rank)

Charlemagne (742–841 CE) was persecuted as a child by his elder brother and fled to Saracen Spain. There under another name he rendered services to the King and converted the daughter to Christianity and secretly arranged to marry her. After further deeds, the youth returned to France and overthrew his former persecutors and assumed the crown.

Each of these legends, constructed to glorify the named hero, exhibits the theme of infant exile and return.

End Note

I cannot leave this topic, however without reference to two currently popular works one written by a scholar of Anglo-Saxon at Oxford**, J.R.R. Tolkien**, who was a devout Catholic, and one written by an unemployed single mother, **J.K. Rowling**. Both of these works reflect the messages we have studied above, the hero and his journey and quest. In one work—Tolkien's 'The Lord of the Rings'—a simple person Frodo Baggins is given a great task, to free Middlearth. He sets out with a companion-helper under the protection of a Wizard, Gandolf.

In the other work—Rowling's 'Harry Potter and …' Harry is an unwanted person who has no living parents, though born of Wizards. He is called to training to combat forces that have an inimical effect on society. Here is an excerpt from a long review of these books:

Both of these works are, fundamentally, Christian works. To begin, the Rings trilogy is profoundly Christian. Tolkien and his colleague C. S. Lewis, author of 'The Screwtape Letters' and one of the most prominent voices for evangelical Christianity of the past century, often discussed the ways in which the Christian faith could be expressed in alternative shapes and forms. They believed that one can communicate the content of Christianity without merely repeating Bible verses, or words lifted from traditional creeds or confessions. And they both set out to create a new literature that would speak to traditional Christians as well as to readers who were alienated from Christianity. Tolkien in particular wanted to create a literature in which the faith was implied rather than imposed, and suggested rather than preached. Of course, the effort to do this may seem both impossible and unnecessary to Christians who identify their faith with certain words or phrases, and believe that there is one and only one way to faithfully communicate Christianity. By contrast, Tolkien saw the need for speaking truth in fresh, new forms, accessible to those who are put off by official church dogma. **In the Rings trilogy, the words "God" or "Christ" never a**ppear, but the reality that these words refer to are communicated in every word and phrase of the text.

First, and most important, is the basic fact that events that transpire in Middle Earth do so according to a lovingly crafted plan, which would be referred to in Christian parlance as "Providence." The suggestion that the "Ring" can be the key to whether good or evil prevails speaks of a universe founded upon certain principles, or as Christians would put it, "created" by a certain God**. Second**, the characters in the narrative are shaped and defined according to their particular role in the unfolding of that plan. Central to the Rings cycle is the notion of Christian heroism, as expressed, for example in both Frodo and Sam, his companion. The true heroes for Tolkien, are not those who excel in qualities of strength or intelligence, but rather exhibit a spiritual depth. The outward manifestation of the inner light is fidelity to a higher cause. At bottom, what makes the hero truly heroic is devotion rather than valor. *The ethic that governs Tolkien's imaginary world is the same one articulated by St. Paul who wrote:* "For now we see in a mirror dimly, but then face to face. Now I know in part; then I shall understand fully, even as I have been fully understood. So faith, hope, love abide, these three; but the greatest of these is love." **Finally**, the universe which Tolkien has created, and is faithfully rendered in the movie that you can now see in a different light, is deeply sacramental in that through its stunning scenery and lavish visual detail, the light comes shining through.

Go see both sets of movies with newly formed eyes.

978-0-595-42021-6
0-595-42021-4

Printed in the United States
139189LV00001B/176/A

9 780595 420216